BECOMING AN INVITATIONAL LEADER

HUMANICS

Becoming an Invitational Leader
A Humanics Trade Group Publication
© 2003 by Brumby Holdings, Inc.
First Edition

Humanics Trade Group Publications are an imprint of and published by Humanics Publishing Group, a division of Brumby Holdings, Inc. Its trademark, consisting of the words "Humanics Trade Group" and the portrayal of a pegasus, is registered in the U.S. Patent and Trademark Office and in other countries.

Brumby Holdings, Inc.
1197 Peachtree St.
Suite 533B
Atlanta, GA 30361
USA

Printed in the United States of America and the United Kingdom

ISBN (Paperback): 0-89334-371-4
ISBN (Hardcover): 0-89334-372-2

Library of Congress Control Number: 2002108265

BECOMING AN INVITATIONAL LEADER

A New Approach to Professional and Personal Success

William W. Purkey, Ed.D.
Betty Siegel, Ph.D.

Humanics Trade Group
Atlanta, GA USA

This book is dedicated with love

to our spouses, Imogene and Joel,

our children,

our children's children,

and also to the extended family

of the International Alliance for Invitational Education.

"Children are the living messages we send to a time we will not see."

--Neil Postman, *The Disappearance of Childhood*

CONTENTS

ACKNOWLEDGMENTS

A favorite saying of ours is that if you see a turtle on a fencepost, you know it didn't get there alone. This truth captures something of the spirit of Invitational Leadership, especially its emphasis on collaboration as the means to personal and professional fulfillment. Whoever helped that turtle to the top of the post-and don't you wish you had been there to see who it was?-is no doubt the kind of person who would also turn to a friend or loved one to quote the words of Walt Whitman: "If you tire, give me both burdens, and rest the chuff of your hand on my hip / And in due time you shall repay the same service to me."

Many people have taken up our burdens over the years. We would like to offer special thanks to our dear colleagues in the International Alliance for Invitational Education-people like David Aspy, William Stafford, John Novak, Jack Schmidt, Charlotte Reed, Eddie Collins, Harvey Smith, Judy Lehr, and so many others who contributed to the theory and practice of Invitational Leadership. More immediately, we thank Craig Watson in the Office of the President at Kennesaw State University for facilitating so well our writing of this book.

We would also like to signal our gratitude to those truly invitational leaders in all fields of endeavor who have been touchstones for us in thinking, living, leading, and writing. In particular, we salute those leaders in education who have been happy and lasting influences: Drs. Virgil Scott Ward, Herman Frick, Ernest Boyer, Art Combs, Parker Palmer, John N. Gardner, Howard Gardner, Sidney Jourard, and Hal G. Lewis. These and other amazing leaders-in education, business, public administration, government, military, not-for-profit work, human resources, counseling and related helping professions-are sustaining examples of what we can accomplish if we work, live, and perform at our best. Many of them are referenced in these pages. Some of them we have been blessed to call colleagues and friends. To all of them, we say thank you for issuing such inspired and inspiring invitations!

Finally, as we explain in chapter six, we must all learn to juggle the glass balls in our lives-family and friends-for they truly are our most precious possessions. We owe the greatest debt of gratitude and love to our own glass balls-our spouses, our children, and our grandchildren-to whom this book is dedicated.

PART I

The Theory of Invitational Leadership

This book is significantly different from many other books on leadership in that it offers a practical and innovative model based on a single theoretical framework. This model shifts from emphasizing control and dominance to one that focuses on connectedness, cooperation, and communication. Based on sound philosophical and psychological assumptions, this model has been tested and successfully applied by leaders in numerous fields, including administration, business, nursing, dentistry, counseling, and other helping professions. Indeed, this model is the basis for the International Alliance for Invitational Education, a network of over one thousand professionals from all fifty states as well as Great Britain, Canada, China, South Africa, and countries throughout Central and South America.

At the heart, Invitational Leadership is a theory of practice that addresses the total environment in which leaders function. As a theory put into practice, it is a powerful process of communicating caring and appropriate messages intended to summon forth the greatest human potential as well as for identifying and changing those forces that defeat and destroy potential.

1

Invitational Leadership cannot be understood if it is thought of as an isolated series of habits, behaviors, or skills. Rather, it is an internal holistic process founded on the four principles of respect, trust, optimism, and intentionality. These guiding principles determine how we invite ourselves and others personally and professionally. What is essential in Invitational Leadership is not the skills we possess, the techniques we use, or the hours we spend working, but the way we balance and live our lives.

Part One, consisting of the first three chapters, explains the underlying theory of Invitational Leadership. Chapter One presents the four principles of the model: respect, trust, optimism, and intentionality. Chapter Two describes the foundations of Invitational Leadership: the perceptual tradition, self-concept theory, and the "whispering self." Chapter Three identifies the four levels of personal and professional functioning: (1) intentionally disinviting, (2) unintentionally disinviting, (3) unintentionally inviting, and (4) intentionally inviting. Together these opening chapters set the stage for Part Two: "The Practice of Invitational Leadership."

CHAPTER ONE:
INTRODUCTION TO
INVITATIONAL LEADERSHIP

Leaders articulate and define what has previously remained implicit or unsaid: then they invent images, metaphors, and models that provide a focus for new attention.

— Walter Bennis and Burt Nanus, *Leaders* (1985, p. 39)

We begin this book with a question you might well ask: Does the world really need another book on leadership? Certainly there are more than enough studies of leadership available—everything from the maddeningly academic to the frustratingly superficial—and indeed by now there is even a book called *Leadership for Dummies* (Kindel & Loeb, 1999). We see no reason to be obscure about this subject, and we wouldn't presume to label as a "dummy" anyone seeking to learn the art of leadership. No, we take up this subject because we think we have discovered through the years a more practical, holistic, and dynamic model of leadership—one that encourages leaders to pursue more joyful and more meaningful personal and professional lives, and to invite their colleagues, family, friends, loved ones, and community to do the same. We call this model *Invitational Leadership*.

3

Most of us tend to think of leadership as something that is exerted by one individual onto others—that is, the leader, having earned a position of dominance and power, begins to issue orders and direct his or her subordinates. No matter how kind and generous they might be toward their associates, such leaders are of the command-and-control variety. The fallacy of such thinking has been documented by Collins (2001), who reported that great companies are not driven by top-down orders. By contrast, Invitational Leadership involves a generous and genuine turning toward others in empathy and respect, with the ultimate goal of collaborating with them on projects of mutual benefit. The emphasis shifts from command and control to cooperation and communication, from manipulation to cordial summons, from exclusiveness to inclusiveness, from *subordinates* to *associates*.

Becoming an Invitational Leader requires a definite point of view. Walter Bennis, one of our more dynamic thinkers on leadership, has defined a leader as one who is guided by an exciting and specific dream and who enrolls others in his or her vision. A classic example of visionary leadership is provided by Mahatma Gandhi, who elevated the hopes and aspirations of many millions of Indians through non-violent means. Invitational Leaders enroll others by summoning them cordially to realize their potential.

A concept like "invitation" is the product of centuries of human effort by those seeking to communicate ideas. This involves shaping, molding, and changing the meanings of words. The word *invite* is a derivation of the Latin word *invito*. It probably began as *vito*, which means to avoid or shun. In early Roman society, *vito* was used to express fear of encroachment by other tribes, and to forbid their entry into Rome. As Rome became a dominant force, its citizens felt more secure and opened their borders to the world. In time the prefix *in-*, meaning "without" or "not," was added, and the word *invito*, meaning "to receive politely," became common and developed into *invite*. So by definition, an invitation is a purposive and generous act by which the inviter seeks to enroll others in the vision set forth in the invitation. From this we derive the term *Invitational Leadership.*

A basic and somewhat radical assumption of Invitational Leadership relates to human motivation. This radical assumption is that there is only one kind of human motivation—an internal and continuous incentive that every person has at all times, in all places, during all activities. *People are always motivated.* In fact, they are never unmotivated. They may not do what we would prefer them to do, but it can never be truly said that they are unmotivated. In thinking invitationally this is a tremendous advantage. Invitational Leaders assume that motivation is a force that comes from within each person. Rather than spending endless amounts of energy and time trying to motivate people, Invitational Leaders seek to unleash each person's intrinsic energy by summoning people cordially to see themselves as capable of tackling tough challenges, overcoming obstacles, and accomplishing great things.

Various books on leadership encourage leaders to "motivate," "shape," "reinforce," "make," "enhance," "turn on," "lift up," "build," "compel," and "empower" people, but this kind of "doing to" language is metaphorically appropriate for working with objects and machines, not people. As well-intended as the authors of these books may be, their writings suggest that they view people as objects. There are dangers in the "objectification" of people who are treated as physical things to be moved here and there. A "doing-to" mentality is the opposite of thinking invitationally. Things are to be used; people are to be invited. From an invitational viewpoint, individuals are able, valuable, and responsible, and are to be treated accordingly. This viewpoint is reflected in such respectful language as "offer," "propose," "present," "encourage," "consider," and "summon cordially." The words we use to describe behaviors influence the ways we behave.

The term "inviting" describes those communicative acts that present something beneficial for consideration. The

Invitational Leader is one who summons associates to higher levels of functioning and presents them with the opportunity to participate in the construction of something of mutual benefit. This "something" ultimately reveals itself in the noble effort to create a better world and to eliminate gross inequalities. This in turn will help to hold society together and sustain human decency. Invitational Leadership presents a fresh paradigm that sees leadership as a force for positive social change. It acknowledges our integrity, our potential, our interdependence, and our responsibility to do good.

Invitational Leaders seek to enroll associates in a vision of greatness—to offer them a vivid and compelling picture of their relatively boundless potential in all areas of worthwhile human endeavor. Invitational Leadership, then, is founded upon certain principles that serve as a conceptual framework to assist leaders in their efforts to communicate their vision and to summon associates to higher levels of optimal life functioning.

In his book *The Leadership Engine*, Noel Tichy (1997) sets forward practices successful leaders perform to communicate their values. These include clear and specific values consistently articulated and reflected upon, embodiment of these values in the leader's own actions, and the continuous encouragement of associates to apply these values to their behavior.

Further support for the importance of values was provided by Stoll and Fink (1996) in their study of leadership in education. They reported that successful leaders depend upon a clear set of values to guide the decisions they make. There are four fundamental values, what we call principles, that give Invitational Leaders direction and purpose. Together, these four principles form a basic set of guiding beliefs that are echoed throughout this book. These are *respect, trust, optimism,* and *intentionality.*

RESPECT

Nothing is more important in Invitational Leadership than respect for people—the belief that we and our associates are able, valuable, and responsible, and should be treated accordingly. Invitational Leadership provides a new vision based on the process of summoning people cordially to move in more democratic, creative, and productive directions through non-coercive means. Central to respect is an appreciation for the rich complexity of each person, coupled with a recognition of the unique value of each culture. Invitational Leaders view diversity as a benefit to the entire group.

As a lesson in the value and richness of diversity, one of the authors had the opportunity to observe a close-order marching drill presented by soldiers of the 82nd Airborne of the United States Army. During the demonstration it was possible to spot the influence of many cultures, including Native American, British, Asian, African, and even that of New Zealand. This is one reason why the American Army, reflecting rich diversity, is considered among the best in the world. Moreover, the amazing diversity of American citizens has been a major factor in the vitality, creativity, and world leadership of the United States of America.

Respect is manifested in such courteous behaviors as civility, politeness, and common courtesy. Waterman and Peters (1988), in their book *In Search of Excellence*, reported that a special characteristic of highly successful companies is the courteous and respectful behavior of their employees. They are good listeners, pay attention to their customers, are courteous, and treat people as adults. Respect is one of eight major characteristics that distinguish excellent companies.

In *Executive Selection: Strategies for Success*, Sessa and Taylor (2000) report that relationship skills are closely connected with leadership ability. Successful leaders take a strong, personal interest in their associates and get results through respectful relationships. Respect is manifested in the leader's promptness in giving credit and expressing appreciation for the caring and appropriate actions of others. It is also manifested in a willingness to make immediate and sincere apologies for inappropriate or uncaring behavior.

When we write of respect we are considering more than good manners and polite behavior. Respect is also manifested in intellectual discourse and a willingness to express vigorous dissent while remaining open to the expressions of others. The importance of respectful discourse is critical to a democratic society. Kingsweel (1994) in his work has demonstrated the strong relationship between good citizenship and respectful civility.

An often overlooked part of respect is caring. Respect reveals itself in caring behavior. It is significant that *cor*, the Latin word for heart, is the basis for the word courage. Inviting comes from courage, and courage comes from caring.

Perhaps the greatest need of any leader is courage. By demonstrating respect through caring and courage, Invitational Leaders summon themselves and others to be able, valuable, and responsible. Caring and its companion, courage, are especially important in Invitational Leadership because they equip leaders with the ability to see what is needed and the strength to overcome obstacles to realize these needs.

Fortunately, courage is contagious. Acting confidently and consistently toward one's goal, and behaving according to the principles of Invitational Education, the leader summons a high level of commitment in others.

Respect is especially important in Invitational Leadership because it is the quality that enables leaders to be a beneficial presence in the lives of human beings. As Max DePree (1989) points out in *Leadership is An Art*, leadership is more tribal than scientific. It is more a weaving of relationships than an amassing of information. What makes this "weaving of relationships" possible is the ability of the leader to take a respectful stance toward colleagues—literally inviting others into a mutually beneficial relationship.

The Invitational Leader is always aware that his or her success depends upon other people, and for this reason respecting others is a crucial element of leadership. The question for the Invitational Leader is not "How can others make me a success?" but rather "How can I summon my colleagues to reach their full potential?" Again, DePree (1989) offers us another way of thinking about this concept: "Leadership is a concept of owing certain things to the institution. It is a way of thinking about institutional heirs, a way of thinking about stewardship as contrasted with ownership" (p. 12). Note the language DePree uses here — *owing, heirs, stewardship* — and imagine what happens to our relationships once we begin to think of ourselves as paying a debt to our colleagues and to the future through our leadership. What happens before all else is that we begin to relate to others *respectfully*.

Throughout his career, John Dewey stressed the importance of respect in human interactions. Dewey maintained that the more democratic the group is, the more the group experience builds on the unique perspectives and interests of its members, and the more the group experience becomes a source of fulfillment for all involved.

A simple but graphic example of respect was provided by a small sign we noticed at the entrance to an antique store:

IF YOU ACCIDENTALLY BREAK AN ITEM, WE
WOULD HOPE THAT YOU MIGHT PURCHASE
AN ITEM OF EQUAL OR GREATER VALUE TO
OFFSET THE COST OF THE BROKEN ITEM.

Compare the above sign with YOU BREAK IT, YOU BOUGHT IT.

In another example, the following sign was posted at the entrance of a department store:

> PLEASE ENJOY YOUR FOOD AND DRINK
> BEFORE SHOPPING WITH US.

The above is a far cry from NO FOOD OR DRINK ALLOWED IN STORE.

A third example was provided by a tire service center:

> CUSTOMERS ARE WELCOME IN THE SHOP AREA. BECAUSE YOUR SAFETY IS IMPORTANT TO US, WE WILL PROVIDE YOU WITH AN ESCORT AND PROPER EYE PROTECTION BEFORE ENTERING. THANK YOU.

This sign makes for a striking comparison with the usual KEEP OUT! warning. Signs are strong indicators of the presence or absence of Invitational Leadership.

A classic model of respect for people and their ideas was provided by Thomas Jefferson. An inventor, architect, musician, scientist, farmer, diplomat, lawyer, surveyor, astronomer, mathematician, anthropologist, and botanist (not to mention author of the *Declaration of Independence*), Jefferson was a living example of what it means to respect people and their ideas. Although he was born into a society that justified terrible slavery, he worked to abolish slavery and to encourage democracy. When Alexander Hamilton and others questioned the ability of men and women to rule themselves, Jefferson never wavered in his respect for the self-directing powers of people to find their own best ways. Although Jefferson grew up and lived in a society that accepted slavery as natural, he recognized the evils of slavery and, within the rigid constraints imposed by the culture, made unsuccessful efforts to eradicate it.

Jefferson's commitment to reason and democratic practice is illustrated by an incident involving the Prussian Ambassador to the United States. When he was President of the young United States, Thomas Jefferson was visited by the

Prussian Ambassador, Baron Alexander Von Humboldt. The Baron entered Jefferson's study and noticed on Jefferson's desk a Federalist Newspaper which featured a scurrilous attack on Jefferson. Baron Von Humboldt asked: "Why do you tolerate such lies? Why don't you shut down the newspaper and have them all arrested?" Jefferson laughed and replied: "Mr. Ambassador, please take this newspaper and put it in your pocket. When you get back to Europe and they ask you whether or not there is freedom in this new nation, please take the paper out of your pocket, show it to your friends, and tell them where you got it." Jefferson believed that if the people made poor decisions, the remedy was not to take away their power but to educate them (Malone, 1972, Wagoner, 1976).

One further comment about respect is that those of us who adopt Invitational Leadership seek to accomplish results without resorting to authoritarian methods. A basic theme of Invitational Leadership is that leaders cannot run roughshod over people. This is stressed by Goleman (2002) and others who have emphasized the power of respect in interpersonal relationships.

An invitation is not a sugar-coated demand. It is a cordial summons to consider something beneficial for acceptance or rejection. True commitment cannot be forced, only volunteered. Behaviors that demean, ignore, or deny the rights of others are judged unacceptable despite any perceived effectiveness or efficiency. Ends do not justify means.

There are times, of course, when something drastic has to be done and done now. Responsibilities go hand in hand with accountability, and penalties in life are unavoidable. But even in extreme circumstances, Invitational Leadership comes into play. How to be an Invitational Leader in difficult situations will be addressed in chapter six.

TRUST

Trust is defined as having confidence in the abilities, integrity, and responsibilities of ourselves and others. Trust is critical to Invitational Leadership because it recognizes the interdependence of human beings. This interdependence is evident when we give a high priority to human welfare, when we view places, policies, programs, and processes as contributing to or subtracting from this welfare, and when we have a willingness to trust one another. In Invitational Leadership, trust is a cooperative, collaborative activity where process is as important as product.

Trust is vital to human endeavor. Consider the many occupations, from fire fighters to military personnel, from commercial airline pilots to medical staff, from mountain climbers to trapeze artists, who must have absolute trust in associates. Without trust, any progress would be extremely difficult. In fact, the level of trust is related to the creation of prosperity in a society. As documented by Fukuyama (1995), in all successful economic societies, communities are united by trust. On the other hand, poor economic performance in a society is related to lack of trust.

As a general rule, trust is created when an organization shares a set of values that creates expectations of regular and honest behavior (Fukuyama, 1995). Further, as Bennis and Nanus (1985) argue, if trust is to be developed in an organization, there must be predictability. Predictability is the capacity to anticipate the behavior of others. Another way of saying this is that organizations without trust would resemble the ambiguous nightmare of Kafka's *The Castle*, where nothing could be certain and nobody could be relied on or held accountable. The ability to predict outcomes with a high probability of success generates and maintains trust.

Trust is established in predictable patterns of action, as opposed to a single act. It is created and maintained through sources identified by Arceneaux (1994). These include *reliability* (consistency, dependability, and predictability), *genuineness* (authenticity and congruence), *truthfulness* (honesty, correctness of opinion, and validity of assertion), *intent* (good character, ethical stance, and integrity), and *competence* (intelligent behavior, expertness, and knowledge.) Trust is established and maintained through these interlocking human qualities, and each reflects Invitational Leadership.

The leader who has established trust throughout his or her organization has come a long way toward ensuring the ultimate success of that organization. Indeed, trust by definition implies dependence on one another. We depend upon each other to tell the truth, as well as to work with each other's best interests in mind. Our dependence on one another also allows for the kind of creativity that can only emerge during collaborative work—what Stephen Covey (1998) in *The Nature of Leadership* calls "the diversity that creates synergy" (p. 105).

A relationship built upon a foundation of trust is much like that formed between sequoia trees. The guides in the Sequoia National Forest, located along the windswept and earthquake-prone Pacific Coast of California, tell visitors a little-known fact about those enormous trees. Growing to over three hundred feet in height and hundreds of tons in weight, the sequoias actually have very shallow root systems. How do the guides account for this phenomenon? Simple: Each sequoia reaches out with its roots to a neighboring tree. Their roots embrace, forming a kind of interlocking network of roots that allows each tree to stand tall and secure. The sequoias provide an instructive example. They stand tall thanks to the support of associates. Built upon a foundation of trust, the Invitational Leader and colleagues embrace each other in seeking to fulfill mutual goals. They stand tall in each other's presence, and they become strong through mutual support.

To nurture this kind of mutual support, the Invitational Leader has a deep responsibility to establish trust as a core value of his or her organization. Indeed, DePree (1989) defines this responsibility as a "covenant" owed by the leader to his or her colleagues: "Leaders owe the organization a new reference point for what caring, purposeful, committed people can be in the institutional setting" (p. 15). There is a certain vulnerability to this stance, but there is also great strength to be found in moving from the command-and-control style of leadership to an invitational style founded on trust. Margaret Wheatly (1992) describes this process in *Leadership and the New Science*, as she learns to give up control in order to form more meaningful relationships: "I want to surrender my care of the universe and become a participating member, with everyone I work with, in an organization that moves gracefully with its environment, trusting in the unfolding dance of order" (p. 23).

Trust also involves trusting ourselves and our own feelings. Hugh Prather (1970), in his classic book *Notes to Myself*, expressed his trust in himself this way: "My intuitive sense of the natural right thing to do under the circumstances, when it is really working, seems somehow to take future events into consideration. I feel 'Do this,' and it is not until afterwards that I can see the sense of it." Invitational Leaders pay careful attention to the faint, whispering, inner voice that is sometimes called intuition. Many of the greatest fundamental successes in modern science were achieved through intuition, hunch, and sudden insight. Where there is trust there is likely to be risk-taking, and where there is risk-taking, there is likely to be creativity and innovation.

OPTIMISM

The belief that people possess untapped potential in all areas of human endeavor is fundamental to Invitational Leadership. A statement made by Norman Cousins on the occasion of his seventieth birthday is worth repeating here: "The most important thing I think I have learned is that human capacity is infinite, that no challenge is beyond comprehension and useful resource. I have learned that the uniqueness of human beings is represented by the absence of any ceiling over intellectual or moral development." Invitational Leaders embrace this optimistic view of human existence and potential: that people are able, valuable, responsible, capable of self-direction, and should be treated accordingly. We optimistically assume that one of the deepest urges of human nature is to be intimately involved in mutually beneficial and caring relationships. What people desire most is to be affirmed in their present worth while being summoned cordially to realize their potential. Invitational Leaders summon associates to become what they are capable of being.

Many research studies have examined the effects of dispositional optimism on psychological well-being. Scheier and Carver (1993) reported a remarkably consistent pattern of findings across studies: "Optimists typically and routinely maintain higher levels of subjective well-being during times of stress than do people who are less optimistic" (27). Scheier and Carver continued: "Research from a variety of sources is beginning to suggest that optimists cope in more adaptive ways than do pessimists. Optimists are more likely than pessimists to take direct action to solve their problems, are more playful in dealing with the adversity they confront, and are more focused on their coping efforts. Moreover, optimists are more likely to accept the reality of the stressful situations they encounter, and they seem intent on growing personally from negative experiences while trying to make the best of bad situations" (pp. 27-28).

To put it another way, optimists are more willing to change, even when they may have concerns about outcomes. The Invitational Leader treats change not as a threat but as a necessary step in personal and professional growth. In *The Nature of Leadership* Stephen Covey (1998) encourages leaders to approach change in precisely this way: "For the effective leader, change is a friend, a companion, a powerful tool, the basis of growth" (p. 58). Encouraging positive change is what

Invitational Leadership is all about.

Compare the spirit of optimism with the glum, pessimistic approach to life represented by Eeyor in Milne's *Winnie the Pooh* (1926): "Eeyor, the old grey donkey, stood by the side of the stream, and looked at himself in the water. 'Pathetic,' he said, 'That's what it is. Pathetic.' He turned and walked slowly down the stream for twenty yards, splashed across it, and walked slowly back on the other side. Then he looked at himself in the water again. 'As I thought,' he said, 'No better from *this* side. But nobody minds, nobody cares. Pathetic, that's what it is'" (p. 72).

Eeyore is always fixated on what is wrong with situations. A second example is also instructive: "Good morning, Eeyore,' said Pooh, 'Good morning, Pooh Bear,' said Eeyore, gloomily, 'if it *is* a good morning, which I doubt.'" Compare Eeyore's gloomy outlook on life with that of Pooh Bear, who is free of preconceptions and open to potentialities. When Eeyore loses his tail, he says: "Someone must have taken it ... how like them." To which Pooh responds, "I, Winnie-The-Pooh, will find your tail for you." (Milne, 1926, p. 44-45). Invitational Leaders could do well by applying the lessons taught from children's books and fables. Believe that life is worth living, and this optimistic belief helps to create the reality.

As Warner (1976) reminds us in his study of great naval commanders, the leader must be ever hopeful. "Shoot pessimists on sight!" Lord Fisher once exclaimed, and the history of leadership makes clear that a great leader will turn in wrath upon anyone who saps confidence in victory (p. 13).

Invitational Leaders work to make the best of situations by modifying negative internal dialogue through the language of optimism. The words we use influence our thoughts, and our thoughts determine our behavior. Using the language of optimism is a characteristic of Invitational Leaders.

Regarding the use of language, Invitational Leaders do not hesitate to use emotionally-charged words like *greatness, spirit, adventure, service, vision, integrity, compassion, loyalty, nobility*, *bravery*, and *gallantry*. Such words, while rarely spoken by many who profess to lead, have the power to establish their own presence. They give us the energy to achieve goals which may be currently considered unachieveable or impossible.

An example of the impact of emotionally-charged words is provided by the writings of Louisa May Alcott:

> Far away there in the sunshine are my highest aspirations. I may not reach them, but I can look up and see their beauty, believe in them, and try to follow where they lead.

Words like *aspirations*, *beauty*, and *believe* represent ardent desires and sincere beliefs. They have the power of Martin Luther King's phrase "*I have a dream*" to make great things come to pass. The individual who believes that he or she can make things happen is probably right, and so is the person who believes that nothing can be done.

Invitational Leaders work to make the best of situations by modifying negative internal dialogue through the language of optimism: "lost" becomes "misplaced," "problem" becomes "situation" or even "opportunity," "no trouble" becomes "my pleasure," "never" becomes "unlikely," "can't" becomes "won't," and "impossible" becomes "difficult." The words we use influence our thoughts, and our thoughts determine our behavior. Using the language of optimism is an important part of Invitational Leadership.

Using the language of optimism is not the same as the current political term "spin," where political "spin doctors" distort information to place politicians in the best possible light. It is different because the language of optimism is accompanied by the principles of respect for people and their intelligence and trust in their abilities to see through manipulative efforts to distort information and deceive people.

A corollary to optimism is perseverance. To think invitationally demands an intentionality that is tirelessly persistent in its stated goal. Leaders are often faced with seemingly immovable barriers. As a result frustration can feed discontent and despair to the point where some leaders give up. Yet challenges, problems, and even impossibilities may be invitations in disguise. Even if everything is working against what should be done, one inviting act has the power to make a profound difference in life events.

It is worth noting here that perseverance often requires change, which usually goes through four states: (1) awareness (that change is possible), (2) understanding (that change is desirable), (3) application (to try a little), and (4) adoption (the way things are done here). Moving from awareness to adoption without taking the intervening steps often leads to action without understanding. Sometimes, the Invitational Leader can be thankful if there is even awareness.

Harriet Beecher Stowe offered this advice on perseverance: "When you get into a tight place and everything goes against you, till it seems you could not hold on a minute longer, never give up then, for that is just the place and time that the tide will turn." The ancient Greeks believed that the gods will save the doomed warrior if he perseveres.

Consider these examples of perseverance: Madelene L'Engle's *A Wrinkle in Time*, and James Joyce's *The Dubliners* were each rejected by over 20 publishing houses, as was the first Dr. Seuss book. It took the inventor of Xerox more than eight years to convince someone with venture capital that his invention was commercially exploitable, and both Decca and Columbia Records turned down recording contracts with the Beatles. A classic example of stick-to-itness is provided by General George Patton (1947) in his book *War as I Knew It*: "Make up your mind on course and direction of action, and stick to it" (p. 5). The message from these examples is that Invitational Leaders do not give up easily; instead, they remain intentionally optimistic.

An optimistic commitment to life within the scope of reason is beautifully stated on an inscription found on a marker along the Aegean Sea:

> A shipwrecked sailor buried on this coast
> Bids you set sail.
> Full many a bark, when we were lost,
> Weathered the gale.

The voice of the dead sailor urges us to be optimistic. When chances are good, take the chance. As basketball players know, one-hundred percent of the shots we do not take will miss the basket. Although we can never be sure of the outcome, we can live our lives with a measure of both optimism and realism. While a pessimist complains about the wind, an optimist hopes it will improve and looks forward to that eventuality. And what does a realist do? He or she adjusts the sail! There is surely a little bit of the optimist inside every realist.

Invitational Leadership is at heart a moral activity, intentionally expressing respect and trust in ourselves and others, personally and professionally. It is both optimistic and realistic. It is not about sugar-coated palliatives regarding the power of positive thinking or about tossing gratuitous compliments and praise at every opportunity. It is about applying a particular theory of democratic practice, and doing so with the fullest and best intentions to nurture a decent and caring society.

INTENTIONALITY

Intentionality is at the very heart of Invitational Leadership. Of the four principles, intentionality plays the paramount role in Invitational Leadership because it is the element that gives any human activity purpose and direction. Respect, trust, and optimism have strength in accordance with the intentionality of the leader. Intentionality is central to the other three elements because it implies a choice and a desire to be respectful, trustworthy, and optimistic.

Human potential can best be realized by places, policies, processes, and programs specifically designed to invite development, and by people who are intentionally inviting with themselves and others, personally and professionally. Indeed, intentionality has been defined as "the structure which gives meaning to experience" (May, 1969, p. 223). May viewed intentionality as the ability of people to link their inner conscious thought with their intentions and overt behavior. By this definition, intentionality is not to be confused with intentions. Intentionality is the dimension which underlies intention. It is our ability to have intentions in the first place.

Csikszentmihalyi (1990) observed that consciousness is "intentionally ordered information." Everything that reaches consciousness is evaluated in terms of its influence on the perceived self. If it is perceived as beneficial, it is accepted; if it has no relationship or influence, it is ignored. If it is viewed as hostile to the perceived self, it is actively defended against. Intentionality is the process of gaining mastery over perceptions. Individuals who are unaware of the power of perceptions have no control over them. As Louis Pasteur noted, "*le hazard ne favorise que les esprits prepares*"—that is, chance favors only the prepared mind. Simply stated, *intentionality is the ordering of our thought processes.*

To act intentionally, with purpose, to act with an aim, is the very essence of Invitational Leadership. The more intentionality we have as leaders, the more accurate our judgments, the more disciplined our commitment to action, and the more decisive our behavior. The leader's energy, vitality, and commitment are directly linked to his or her intentionality.

An extreme example of intentionality was provided by the response of a Hollywood Agent who was told by a movie producer to "Get lost and don't come back for ten years." The Agent responded: "Morning or afternoon?" Invitational

Leadership requires a disciplined commitment to sustained action, to march confidently towards a vision of a better world.

In his book *The Reckoning*, Halberstram (1986) provides a disturbing account of the decline and fall of Detroit, Michigan as the world's leader in the manufacture of automobiles. The top management in automobile manufacturing lacked a commitment to quality. He pointed out that true quality in a product demands an intentionality that begins at the very top, then seeps down into the middle and lower levels of management, and then to the assembly line workers. Without intentionality from the top down, organizations are likely to fail.

Consider the lack of intentionality found in the dialogue between Alice and the Cat in Lewis Carroll's *Through the Looking Glass*:

> Alice: Which way should I go?
> Cat: That depends on where you are going.
> Alice: I don't know where I am going!
> Cat: Then it doesn't matter which way you go!

Invitational Leaders enroll followers in the design and development of places, policies, programs, and processes that lead to ultimate aims. An aim implies an orderly activity in which the order consists of the completing of an intentional process. Invitational Leadership is based on a guiding image of the desirable course of action, coupled with a disciplined commitment to action. When the leader's aims are clear, decision making becomes easier. In addition, leaders who perceive significance and meaning in their aims are far more likely to enlist others in their guiding vision. This vision invites people to think in creative ways and to act intentionally with the future in mind. Aims are vital, for they are manifestations of intentionality.

In thinking about the importance of a guiding vision, consider the actions of a lion on the hunt. Birds and other animals that are preyed upon are constantly looking around, eyes darting here and there. The lion locks in with a steely, unblinking gaze. There are times when thinking like an Invitational Leader means to go "lion-eyed." A guiding image, when expressed in passionate ways, has the ability to summon others to enroll in the leader's vision and to take them to higher levels of functioning.

Erich Fromm (1956) explained the value of an overarching guiding image with these words: "I shall never be good at anything if I do not do it in a disciplined way: anything I do only if 'I'm in the mood' may be a nice or amusing hobby, but I shall never become a master of that art" (p. 108). Abraham Lincoln's rule for greatness was that whatever he had to do, he would put his whole mind to it and hold it there until that particular task was done. Great leaders, such as Lincoln, realize their greatness only after they prioritize their goals, settle on the most important, and then move heaven and earth to accomplish them.

An astonishing example of one person's intentionality — for good or for ill — took place in 1916, when Leon Trotsky was in New York. Trotsky, then known by his real name, Leib Davydovich Bronstein, hung around Broadway theatres and did odd jobs. One day he went to his friends and announced that he was returning to Russia. When asked why he was going, he replied: "To overthrow the government." This zealous intentionality — this claritry of purpose — was a critical factor in the Russian Revolution and the birth of Communism.

A valuable aspect of intentionality is that it helps Invitational Leaders to generate choices in a given situation. It allows us to develop plans, act on them, and evaluate the effects of these actions. Invitational Leadership maintains that human potential can best be realized by people who create places, policies, programs, and processes (the five powerful "P's" to be presented in chapter five) that are so purposefully welcoming as to create a total environment in which each person is cordially summoned to develop optimally, both personally and professionally. The intentionally inviting leader, then, always makes choices with others in mind, as respectful, trusting relationships dictate. When we make choices that benefit the entire organization, honoring the covenant we have established with our colleagues, then we lead, as Stephen Covey (1998) writes, "in ways that release human potential rather than trying to control behavior" (p. 93).

The Invitational Leader is unique in asking others to meet their goals *as a condition* of his or her own success. This is not merely a by-product of invitational theory. On the contrary, encouraging others in their quest for self-fulfillment is embedded in the principles of Invitational Leadership. Leadership, then, becomes a *mutual* commitment between colleagues, rather than a series of orders issued from the top down. As this chapter has maintained, Invitational Leadership is based upon the guiding principles of respect, trust, optimism, and intentionality. These principles serve as guideposts:

- Respect is measured by how we treat ourselves and others.
- Trust encourages collaborative risk-taking and creative problem solving.
- Optimism is evidenced by positive and realistic expectations.
- Intentionality gives direction and purpose to our decisions and makes action possible.

Finally, it is important to remember that Invitational Leadership has a significant personal component. To be truly inviting toward others, after all, we must be inviting towards ourselves. We recall the famous questions Carl Sandburg (1948) asks of himself in his book *Remembrance Rock*: "Who am I? Where do I come from? Where am I going?" These questions should be asked and answered by every Invitational Leader, for they can help us begin to define our stories and outline our visions for the future. They will also inevitably lead us to an all-important fourth question, which deserves our utmost attention: "What is my meaning, and how can I contribute to the meaning of others?" For the Invitational Leader, answering that question is part of a lifelong process of joy, discovery, and human service.

Chapter Two:
Foundations of
Invitational Leadership

Leadership is a matter of how to be, not how to do. We spend most of our lives mastering how to do things, but in the end it is the quality and character of the individual that defines the performance of great leaders.

> —Frances Hesselbein, *Leader to Leader* (1999, p. xii)

We intend the statement with which we closed Chapter One — that Invitational Leaders must necessarily ask themselves the question of what gives them meaning and purpose— to be taken quite literally. Indeed, answering this question helps Invitational Leaders craft narratives of their personal and professional lives, stories that evolve as their ideas change—as they themselves change—revealing ever-new applications for their careers and collegagues. Further, and perhaps most importantly, asking and answering such a question should be a natural extension of a continuous internal dialogue. This dialogue is a key component of what it requires to become an Invitational Leader. It is also central to the development of a positive *and* realistic self-concept.

Any theory of leadership is based on certain beliefs or "cornerstones" regarding what people are like and what they might become. The three cornerstones of Invitational Leadership are the perceptual tradition, self-concept theory, and the "whispering self." Considering these cornerstones will help us to answer another question: How does the leader learn to think invitationally?

Becoming an Invitational Leader requires that a leader become more consciously aware of his or her self and, by so doing, take responsibility for how he or she defines that self. After all, if we perceive ourselves to be lacking in some fundamental leadership quality, then surely we will fail to move others to join our cause. But if we can learn to speak invitationally to ourselves—if how we speak to ourselves helps us define a largely optimistic self-concept—then the sense of possibility in our personal and professional lives will expand exponentially.

The first step in becoming an Invitational Leader is to become aware of, and to monitor, our perceptions. Our perceptions of ourselves, others, and the world are so real to us that we seldom pause to question them. Yet, human behavior is always a product of how we see ourselves and the situations in which we are involved. Although this fact seems obvious, the failure of people everywhere to comprehend it is responsible for much of human misunderstanding, maladjustment, conflict, and loneliness. In Invitational Leadership, being aware of, and questioning, our own perceptions is the first step in a re-visioning and re-calibrating of our relationships and responsibilities.

In Walker Percy's novel *The Moviegoer* (1961), narrator Binx Bolling discusses what he calls "repetitions"—"the re-enactment of past experience toward the end of isolating the time segment which has lapsed in order that it, the lapsed time, can be savored of itself and without the usual adulteration of events that clog time like peanuts in brittle" (p. 69). In other words, by recreating the past for himself, Binx is able to give it heightened meaning by the awareness he exercises through the recreation. This is but one of the ways Binx engages experience deliberately and thoughtfully. For instance, he might insist upon seeing a favorite movie in the exact manner in which he saw it the first time—even to the point of sitting in the same seat. By becoming hyper-aware of his actions, he avoids the general devaluation of repetitive experience. Or, as he puts it, he refuses to be defeated by the "malaise" of unquestioned existence.

Binx's existential approach to things can help us understand how leaders learn to think invitationally by first becoming aware of the possibility of doing so. Inspired by the knowledge of this possibility, Invitational Leaders are able to step outside of themselves and observe their behavior more clearly, reevaluate their perceptions, and question how their actions and words become part and parcel of their larger vision of the world. Thus, Invitational Leaders defeat the "malaise" of unquestioned existence, turning toward more joyful, thoughtful, and meaningful personal and professional lives. This process begins with a deeper understanding of those three cornerstones of Invitational Leadership: the perceptual tradition, self-concept theory, and the "whispering self."

THE PERCEPTUAL TRADITION

The perceptual tradition is a way of understanding human behavior that includes all the ways in which we as humans are viewed as we normally view ourselves. The term *perceptual* refers not only to the senses but also to meanings — the personal significance of an event for the person experiencing it. These meanings extend far beyond sensory receptors to include such personal experiences as feelings, desires, aspirations, hopes, as well as opinions about ourselves, others, and the world.

The starting point of the perceptual tradition is the assumption that we are conscious agents in the process of our own development. We experience, interpret, construct, decide, act, and are ultimately responsible for our actions. Behavior is understood as a product of the way we see ourselves and the situations in which we find ourselves. Each individual is seen as a conscious agent in the process of his or her own development.

The focus of this book does not permit a proper recognition of the many scholars from numerous disciplines who have contributed to the perceptual tradition, but we would be remiss not to acknowledge William James's description of consciousness (1890), George Herbert Mead's perspective on the social nature of perception (1934), Art Combs and Donald Snygg (1959) with their perceptual psychology, Carl Rogers' emphasis on people as always in the process of becoming (1974), and, more recently, Albert Bandura's social cognitive theories (1994). The contributions of these and other scholars and researchers continue to enrich our understanding of the power of perception in human affairs.

The perceptual tradition stands in contrast to other approaches that seek to understand human behavior by depicting it as basically a complex bundle of stimuli and responses, the product of a host of unconscious urges, or the result of genetic predispositions. In the perceptual tradition, primary importance is given to how people see themselves, others, and the world. Because of this emphasis on understanding people as they normally see things, the perceptual tradition seems well-suited as a cornerstone for Invitational Leadership.

Three assumptions of the perceptual tradition have particular meaning for Invitational Leadership: behavior is determined by perceptions, perceptions are learned, and perceptions can be reflected upon and modified.

BEHAVIOR IS DETERMINED BY PERCEPTIONS

The perceptual tradition seeks to explain why people do the things they do by postulating that human behavior is determined by, and pertinent to, the phenomenal field of the experiencing person at the moment of acting. In other words, each individual behaves according to how the world appears at that instant. From this vantage point there is no such thing as illogical behavior—each person is behaving in the way that makes the most sense to him or her at a particular moment. What may seem *from an external point of view* as counter-productive and even self-destructive is only an inadequate understanding of what the world looks like from the viewpoint of the perceiving person at that moment of action.

When Richard Nixon proclaimed, "I am not a crook," and Sally Fields shouted, "You like me, you *really* like me!" at the Academy Awards, they received heavy ridicule from the press. Yet, at the moment of action, both Richard Nixon and Sally Fields were stating the best and safest things that came to mind based on their perceptions at the moment of action. No matter how strange or counter-productive the behavior of another person may appear, *from that person's perception at the moment of action*, the behavior is seen as preferable to other actions he or she might take. We perceive what is relevant to our purposes and make our choices accordingly.

Fortunately, each person's perceptual field can be continually enriched, expanded, and modified. The ideas that individuals can enhance their perceptions, and that their perceptual fields are capable of incalculable expansion and enrichment, serve as major reasons and justifications for Invitational Leadership. This optimistic belief provides something to continually appreciate and reach for, a coming together for creative and worthwhile purposes that can extend human experiences. This allows Invitational Leaders to enroll others in a shared, mutually inspiring vision of the future.

PERCEPTIONS ARE LEARNED

Through myriad encounters with the world, particularly those with significant others, we develop certain fundamental perceptions that serve as organizing filters for making sense of the world. Without such a filtering system, we would be relentlessly bombarded by unrelated stimuli. Thus, perceptions serve as a reference point for behavior. Invitational Leadership is based on an understanding of, and respect for, peoples' perceptual worlds. These perceptual worlds are not to be taken lightly, for they provide insights into human behavior.

Our perceptual worlds are formed in three general ways. The first is through a traumatic or ecstatic event. A marriage, the joyous arrival of a baby, career successes or failures, an illness, retirement, the loss of a loved one, can have such impact that our perceptual world is forever changed. Imagine the impact of a physician saying: "Your heart is not as strong as we would like it to be" or "I'm afraid your tests came back positive." Just imagine receiving a registered letter informing you that you have won thirty million dollars. Such information can turn our perceptual world upside down.

The second way that perceptions change is through a professional helping relationship, such as spiritual guidance, medical treatment, or professional counseling. We have all witnessed individuals who, through a religious conversion, medical or dental treatment, or professional counseling seem to change their perceptions of themselves, others, and the world. Professional counseling or psychotherapy can be a tremendous help for some individuals by assisting them to reevaluate and reorganize their perceptual worlds.

The third and by far the greatest influence on perceptions takes place with repeated everyday experiences and consistent events. Gitlow & Gitlow (1987) demonstrated that in business, workers who are consistently encouraged to participate in decision-making processes, or who are repeatedly excluded from such actions, will eventually see themselves as valued participants or mindless functionaries to a system. Everything that happens to us, good or bad, big or small, decent or indecent has a life-long influence on the ways we perceive ourselves, others, and the world.

One further characteristic of our perceptual world is that it is a life-long process of learning. What we choose to perceive is determined by past experiences as mediated by present purposes and future expectations. Of all contemporary theories and models of leadership, none depends more on individual perceptions than does Invitational Leadership. Because perceptions are learned, they offer infinite capacity for positive change and the realization of human potential.

PERCEPTIONS CAN BE REFLECTED UPON

The ability to examine and monitor our perceptions is essential to Invitational Leadership. Being aware of past and present perceptions and being able to imagine future possibilities permit the development of a deeper level of understanding of self, others, and the world. As Csikszentmihalyi (1993) pointed out, reflection can lead a person to develop a more differentiated and integrated self, that is, a personality with many interests creatively harmonized.

Reflection also provides optimism because there is no inevitable future as long as we have the power to examine our lives. Although we cannot change the past, we can change our perceptions of previous events and consequently open more possibilities for the future. Invitational Leadership is more than "I feel"; it is also "I think," "I know," "I reflect," "I monitor," and "I imagine."

So far, we have emphasized that people behave according to how they see things. We explained that these perceptions are learned and can be reflected upon. Now we come to that paramount perception of personal existence: the self-concept.

SELF-CONCEPT

The concept of self has dominated the thinking of American scholars for many decades. In their review of the literature regarding self, Banaji and Prentice (1994) reported finding more than 5,000 books, monographs, and articles on the subject. Obviously, our overview of self-concept will be limited and restricted to its relationship to Invitational Leadership.

Of all perceptions, none seems to affect our search for personal significance and identity more than our self-concept— our awareness of our own personal existence and how we fit into the world. Some theorists (Combs, Avila & Purkey, 1978) have maintained that the maintenance, protection, and enhancement of the perceived self (one's own personal existence as viewed by oneself) is the basic motive behind all human behavior. Use of this assumption, organized into what is generally known as self-concept theory, helps to clarify and integrate seemingly unrelated aspects of human behavior. For example, individuals who see themselves as leaders are likely to respond by providing direction in difficult situations, just as soldiers who see themselves as defeated are likely to run from battle. The dynamics are the same, even if the resulting behaviors are sharply different.

One of the most interesting aspects of self-concept is that it has an internal integrity. If a new conception is congruent with beliefs already present in the self-concept, it is easily assimilated. If the new conception has no relevance, it is ignored; and if it is in opposition with other beliefs already present, it is actively repulsed. This organized self is worth considering more closely.

THE ORGANIZED SELF

Most researchers of self-concept agree that a person's self-concept has a generally stable quality that is characterized by internal orderliness and harmony. It is not simply a hodgepodge of cognitions and feelings. The self-concept is orchestrated and balanced, centered on the "I" that represents immediate awareness of existence. In addition to the "I," the self-concept contains smaller units. These can be thought of as "sub-selves" and represent the self-as-object. These are the varied and myriad "me's" that are the objects of our self-perceptions. Each of the "me" sub-selves contains its own balance and voice, and each influences, and is in turn influenced by, the global self-concept.

During most of the previous century, as reported by Campbell, Assanand, and DiPaula (2000), self-concept was viewed as a unitary, monolithic entity, usually centered on self-esteem. In contrast, contemporary thinking sees self-concept as a multifaceted, dynamic, and many-layered construct of amazing complexity. As Somerset Maugham (1944) noted in *The Razor's Edge*, many individuals live within us, often in uneasy companionship with one another.

Each person maintains countless perceptions regarding his or her personal existence, and each perception is internally orchestrated with all the others. It is this generally stable and organized quality of self-concept that gives consistency to the human personality. The organized quality of self-concept has corollaries:

- Self-concept requires consistency, stability, and tends to resist change. If the self-concept changed readily, the individual would lack a consistent and dependable personality.
- At the heart of self-concept is the self-as-doer, the "I" which is distinct from the self-as-object, the various "me's." This allows the person to reflect on past events, analyze present perceptions, and shape future experiences.
- The more central a particular belief is within one's self-concept (the closer the "me" to the "I") the more resistant the person is to changing that belief.

To picture the global self-concept with its internal symmetry, consider the following figure and imagine that the large spiral represents the organized unity of one's self-concept. The numerous "me" sub-selves can be roughly divided into *attributes* (strong, tall, loyal, short, bright, young, bashful, friendly, faithful, trustworthy, responsible, loyal, helpful, sexy, etc.) and *categories* (student, leader, husband, mother, atheist, athlete, spouse, Muslim, Jew, Christian, homosexual, veteran, American, etc.). These perceived attributes and categories are often linked (bright student, loyal American, faithful spouse, responsible administrator, etc.) and are internally positioned in a hierarchical order. This order is critical, for it gives meaning and stability to the self.

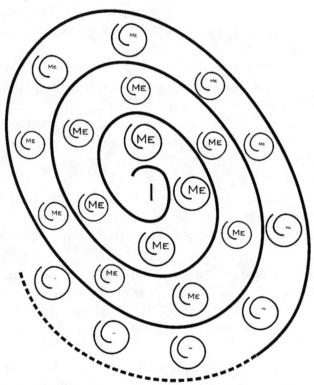

Each person's self-concept contains countless me's, but not all are equally significant. Some are highly important and are close to the center of the self-concept. Other me's are less central and are located toward the periphery. The me's closest to the "I" have the most influence on daily functioning and whisper with the greatest authority. In other words, they "have the king's ear."

It may be helpful to think of the self-concept as a stabilizing lake. This lake is constantly fed by a river of experience that flows into the lake at one end and exits at the other. The river of me's can flow into the self-concept lake rapidly or slowly, depending on life experiences, and can provide much or little fresh water. In the healthy personality, the river dependably provides the lake a manageable number of fresh me's, whereas outmoded me's are flushed out of the lake and down the river. When this life-long process of renewal and development is interrupted, and little water is allowed to enter or leave, the lake becomes stagnant. Conversely, if too much water enters or leaves the lake, it becomes flooded or drained, unpredictable, and provides too little protection against the vagaries of life. When too many me's strive for attention, the leader can lose self-direction and integrity. Where there are too few me's, the individual begins to lose his or her identity and even his or her perceived existence.

The emerging research on self-concept is so vast that this chapter will examine only two aspects of self-concept that relate to the process of becoming an Invitational Leader: the development of self-concept and self-concept as guidance system. Together, these two aspects set the stage for the central player in becoming an Invitational Leader, the "whispering self."

DEVELOPMENT OF SELF

No one is born with a self-concept. The development and structure of self-awareness is a lifelong research project. It is a continuous process of learning. By experiencing the world through countless inviting and disinviting interactions we gradually develop a theory of personal existence. Thanks to myriad interactions with the world, a self-concept is forged, complete with a complex hierarchy of attributes and categories.

The ingredients of self-concept are primarily social, obtained through myriad interactions with persons, places, policies, programs, and processes (the five powerful P's to be addressed in chapter five). Repeated experiences, positive or negative, have a profound effect on the self. W. Somerset Maugham (1944) expressed this gradual process beautifully in *The Razor's Edge*:

> For men and women are not only themselves; they are also the region in which they were born, the city apartment or the farm in which they learned to walk, the games they played as children, the old wives' tale they overheard, the food they ate, the schools they attended, the sports they followed, the poems they read, and the God they believed in. (p. 2)

Everything that happens to us happens forever. Although it is impossible to change the past, it is possible to change our perceptions of past experiences, control our present activities, and imagine and act on future possibilities.

SELF-CONCEPT AS GUIDANCE SYSTEM

As we've seen, self-concept is a complex, continuously active system of subjective and learned beliefs regarding our personal experience. It guides behavior and enables us to assume particular roles in life. Rather than initiating activity, self-concept serves as a perceptual filter and guides the direction of behavior. This "moderator variable" serves as the reference point for behavior. We act in accordance with the ways we have learned to see ourselves. From a lifetime of studying our own actions and those of significant others, we acquire expectations about what things "fit" with our self-concept already in place. As mentioned earlier, if a new perception is consistent with past experiences already incorporated into our self-concept, we easily accept and assimilate the new perception. If the new experience contradicts those already incorporated, we will probably reject it. We tend to incorporate only that which is congenial to the self-concept already in place.

To understand the active nature of self-concept, it helps to imagine it as a gyrocompass, a continuously active system that dependably points to the "true north" of a person's perceived existence. This guidance system not only shapes the ways a person views him or herself, others, and the world, but it also serves to direct action and enables each person to take a consistent "stance" in life. Rather than viewing self-concept as the cause of behavior, it is better to understand it as the gyrocompass of human personality, providing consistency in personality and direction for behavior. This consistency is perhaps most important in relation to internal dialogue—the ways we bolster our self-concept through conversations with the "whispering self."

THE WHISPERING SELF

A third vital cornerstone for Invitational Leadership is a particular thought process which we have named the whispering self. This inner voice is the soundless, inner speech that appears in our head the moment we think about something (it seems impossible to think without thinking about something!). It is this internally audible, hushed voice that we listen to in our heads, which in turn influences what we do as leaders.

According to Sokolov (1972), in all instances, people think, remember, and imagine through the use of private conversation: "Inner speech is nothing but speech to oneself, or concealed verbalization, which is instrumental in the logical processing of sensory data, in their realization and comprehension within a definite system of concepts and judgments" (p. 1). Leaders who are aware that they talk to themselves are in a much better position to monitor and alter their inner voices.

Those who are unaware of the whispering self have lost control of it. It is vital to be aware of our internal dialogue and to know where these voices lead.

The whispering self is the meaning-making narrator who at every waking moment of our lives tells us who we are and what we should be about. In attempting to solve problems, make decisions, select a course of action, or understand a situation, we enter into internal dialogue with ourselves. During these inner conversations we look at options, consider their results, and then select what appears to be the best and safest course of action based on our internal constructions. Sometimes these constructions can be counter-productive. The following story was provided by our friend Bill Stafford:

> A young man was driving his girlfriend home to the suburbs after an evening out. On his return trip back into the city, he had a flat tire in a remote section of the highway. When he went to get the car jack, he remembered he had taken it out of the car and had not replaced it. He recalled that there was a farm house about a half-mile away, and even though it was late at night he decided to walk to the farm house to borrow a jack from the farmer. As he walked he kept talking to himself about how angry the farmer would be and how dumb he felt for even asking. His self-talk continued as he walked up the path to the front door. He knocked on the door loudly, and the upstairs room lit up. The farmer leaned out the window and shouted: "What do you want?" The young man's reply was immediate: "Keep your damned jack! I'll figure out another way to fix my tire."

Internal dialogue can be productive or counter-productive.

As explained by Helmstetter (1986), all of us talk to ourselves all the time. We are thinking machines that never shut down: "At times our self-talk comes in feelings that can't quite be put into words. At other times it comes in little flashes, flickers of thought which never quite catch fire or glow bright enough or last long enough to become ideas, clearly thought out and understood" (p. 36). *It is this inner voice that allows us to respond to and actively manipulate the environment, internally and externally.*

The more intentional our thinking, as measured by clearly articulated internal dialogue, the more likely it is to be acted upon. This hypothesis has been supported by the research of Hockaday, Purkey, and Davis (2000), who reported that by re-framing general internal cognitions into clearly stated internal dialogue, individuals are in a better position to reach their goals and are more likely to do so.

Surprisingly, internal dialogue is that part of human consciousness that has been neglected by those who have written about leadership. Far more books have been written about understanding and controlling the outer world than on how to understand and control the inner self. The fact that internal cognitions serve as a guide for action has been largely overlooked. The whispering self seeks to fill this void. *Invitational Leadership is in large part the product of internal dialogue regarding what we say to ourselves about ourselves, others, and the world.*

DEFINING THE WHISPERING SELF

Many constructs have been used to define the whispering self: "attributions," "defense mechanisms," "verbal mediations," "cognitive mediators," and "beliefs," to name a few. And many names have evolved to describe this hushed inner voice, including "self-talk," "internal dialogue," "inner-conversations," "self-referent thought," "concealed verbalizations," "private speech," "intro-communication," "inner voice," "personal cognitions," "self-statements," and "covert conversation." But whatever term we use to describe this inner speech, it is clear that the whispering self is a vital part of the total thinking process in human consciousness. It arises the moment we think of something, usually with the aid of language we articulate to ourselves.

Castaneda (1972), in his book *A Separate Reality*, explains the nature of the whispering self this way: "The world is such and such or so-and-so because we tell ourselves that is the way it is . . . you talk to yourself. You're not unique in that. Everyone of us does that. We carry on internal talk . . . in fact we maintain our world with our internal talk" (p. 218). In a very special way each person is both subject and object. The whispering self is both speaker and listener.

A graphic description of how the whispering serves as both subject and object, speaker and listener, was provided by Steven Callahan (1986), who was adrift for seventy-six days on a tiny float following the sinking of his sailboat. Here is how Callahan, alone in a vast ocean, described talking to and listening to himself: "Maintaining discipline becomes more difficult each day. My fearsome and fearful crew mutter mutinous misgivings within the fo'c's'le of my head. Their spokesman yells at me. 'Water, Captain! We need more water. Would you have us die here, so close to port? What is a pint or two? We'll soon be in port. We can surely spare a pint....' 'Shut up!' I order. 'We don't know how close we are, might have to last to the Bahamas. Now, get back to work'" (p. 283). This saga describes how a brave man's determined intentionality in the face of insurmountable hardships leads to eventual rescue.

The way we use language — and the language we use — gives structure to our perceptual worlds. Although thinking can occur without language, the words we use greatly enhance thinking and influence behavior. Simply stated, *the way to change the self is to change the self's internal dialogue.*

Leaders talk to themselves, and this private conversation has a profound impact on what they accomplish. Although the whispering self is based on beliefs, it is different in that it has a "here and now" immediate awareness quality. This construct is based on Vygotsky's (1978) theory concerning the internationalization of dialogue as inner speech. Internalized self-talk is thought itself, a theory supported by research (e.g., Butler, 1981; Ellis, 1958, 1962, 1976, 1979; Markus & Nurius, 1986; Meichenbaum 1977, 1985).

Because internal dialogue is the pervasive product of all life experiences, and typically speaks in hushed tones, most people are unaware of its powerful impact on behavior. Yet this inner voice is a potent force for good and ill, for it guides and controls overt behavior. As Csikszentmihalyi (1990) explained, "People who learn to control inner experience will be able to determine the quality of their lives, which is as close as any of us come to being happy" (p. 2). It is thought escaping into the open where it can be crystallized into recognizable self-talk and evaluated for its positive or negative messages. By listening and controlling this subtle inner narration, Invitational Leadership reveals itself.

HEALTHY AND UNHEALTHY WHISPERS

The whispering self can be our dear friend or mortal enemy. No one is immune to this constructive or destructive voice. Sometimes this hushed inner voice is accurate and rational. At other times it speaks in innuendo, half-truths, and gets lost in irrationality.

HEALTHY WHISPERS.

In a healthy person the internal whispers are highly beneficial. They murmur of success, assurance, fulfillment, and provide a large measure of control over both feelings and actions. Scholars who have written about the nature of the self generally agree that individuals who define themselves in essentially positive ways tend to be open to experience, are more willing to disclose their feelings, and face the world with confidence and assurance. In the healthy individual this positive inner voice is moderated by realistic assessment. An example of positive *and* realistic internal dialogue was shared by a friend:

> I used to think that I was a failure if I did not have a big home, fine car, and money in the bank. Now I realize that I may never have these things, and that's O.K. I have many other things that make me a success, including good health, dear friends, and a loving family.

Another friend commented:

> After not getting a new position, I became very depressed. I felt that I must have done something wrong during the interview not to have gotten the promotion. I kept thinking to myself that I had messed up. My wife suggested that it is entirely possible that I could have had a great interview and still not have gotten the position. Perhaps the person chosen just had more experience. This thought helped me to think about the situation in a whole new light.

Growing numbers of research studies have identified the beneficial effects of positive belief systems manifested in self-talk. The research of Scheier and Carver (1992), Seligman (1990), and others suggests that an optimistic belief system results in better academic performance in the classroom, better performance on the athletic field, and better physical health.

A delightfully optimistic approach to life was portrayed in *Life With Father* by Clarence Day: "Father declared he was going to buy a new plot in the cemetery, a plot all for himself. 'And I'll buy on a corner,' he added triumphantly, 'where I can get out!' Mother looked at him, startled but admiring and whispered to me, 'I almost believe he could do it'" (pp. 257-258). Father's upbeat, optimistic outlook on life and beyond serves as an example of invitational thinking in action.

Here are some examples of healthy self-talk:

> "There are some things that I'm not good at."
> "I enjoy challenges."
> "I like the way I look."
> "I trust my feelings."
> "I enjoy working in groups."
> "I have a good memory."
> "I like to volunteer."
> "I'm a responsible person."
> "I've got a good head on my shoulders."
> "I'm optimistic about the future."
> "I find some things difficult."
> "Most people like me."
> "I respect myself."

These comments reflect a positive and realistic view of one's existence. The voice of the self speaks of positive capabilities, coupled with reasonable cautions against being overly optimistic.

UNHEALTHY WHISPERS.

The unhealthy internal voice discourages feelings of confidence and efficacy. This lurking voice can inform us that things are more difficult than they really are while reminding us that we lack the ability to understand and solve problems. It speaks of fear, anxiety, worthlessness, and defeat.

According to Firestone (1997), "Everyone has negative voices — we would not be human without them, but people who are self-destructive have negative voices that dominate their thinking and block the ability to think positively or even rationally. These voices create a person who is essentially turned against oneself. When faced with failure, rejection, illness, loss, or shame, this person has the potential to take action against himself or herself" (p. 7). In the extreme case of suicide, this self-hatred reaches epic proportions. As Shakespeare writes in *MacBeth*, "Foul whisperings are abroad." A foul inner voice can suggest that life is pointless and that the individual is powerless to do anything about it. As important as is positive and realistic internal dialogue, *it is even more important to be aware of the damage inflicted by negative and distorted inner conversations.*

In the field of medicine, the axiom is "First do no harm." In invitational thinking, the axiom is "Eliminate the negative and distorted." Many people tell themselves that they cannot learn, assert, or succeed, even when such things are not objectively true. They encounter difficulties because they are incapable of telling themselves that they can succeed. The presence of negative and distorted self-talk establishes limits and barriers to performance, and these limits and barriers are as "real" as this book.

Listen to the voice of one young man in therapy: "Doubting myself has become a way of life for me. When I turn in a paper I tell myself it's no good. When I ask a girl for a date, I know I'll be turned down. When I apply for a job, I know I won't get it." Such negative self-talk often becomes a self-fulfilling prophecy. Individuals who expect rejection, failure, and defeat become their own worst enemies.

The whispering self has profound effects not only on social behavior but also on biology. Research by Kiecolt-Glaser, Ricker, Messick, Speicher, Garner, and Glaser (1984, a & b) documented the connections between physical immune functions and self-definitions. Working to alter faulty, irrational, or negative self-talk is an important prerequisite not only for leadership but for a healthy life as well.

Imagine the whispering self of an aspiring leader who lacks confidence in himself or herself:

"I'm always putting my foot in my mouth."

> "I can't carry a tune in a bucket."
> "I never know what to say."
> "I can never remember names."
> "I've never been any good with numbers."
> "I have no patience."
> "I can't use computers."
> "I don't have a head for math."
> "I can't stop smoking."
> "I'm not good at taking tests."
> "I can't speak in public."
> "I don't think people like me."
> "I can't dance, I have two left feet."
> "I can't sing, I have a tin ear."
> "I never have enough time."
> "I wish I were better looking."
> "I'm so clumsy."
> "I never win anything."
> "I'd lose my head if it weren't tied on."
> "I'm all thumbs."

It would be difficult if not impossible to achieve much of anything while listening to an inner voice filled with pessimism, self-doubt, and even self-hatred. The language we use internally forms the structure of our consciousness. Changing the ways we speak to ourselves internally changes the very meaning of our existence.

A classic example of "distorted" and self-defeating thinking was provided by Ken Kesey (1962) in *One flew over the cuckoo's nest*:

> "Man, you're talking like a fool! You mean to tell me that you're gonna' sit back and let some old blue-haired woman talk you into being a rabbit?"
> "Not talk me into it, no. I was born a rabbit. Just look at me. I simply need the nurse to make me happy with my role."

"You're no damned rabbit." (p. 62)

By accepting ourselves as a rabbit, or "loser," "clumsy," "ugly," "stupid," "lazy," "unlucky," or "incompetent," our inner voice becomes its own defender, regardless of how ultimately self-defeating the defense may be. The defense against failure is to accept oneself as a failure. The negative voice declares that it is better not to try than to try and be embarrassed or humiliated. By not trying, we maintain some sort of control. This strategy of withholding effort to maintain some sense of self-worth has been documented by the research of Berglas (1985), Covington (1992), and others.

To illustrate how the whispering self can function in positive and realistic ways, consider the following description of internal dialogue provided by one of our doctoral students:

> I often talk to myself in two ways. First, I talk out arguments with myself before I present them to other people. This helps me organize my thoughts and, I hope, appear more polished when I present my thoughts to others. Second, I often 'play out' difficult situations afterwards to better understand what went wrong in the interaction. In the privacy of my mind, I can say what I should have said at the time and did not. It's almost like talking to a friend.

In everyday life, we formulate various courses of action, select what appears to be the most self-enhancing, and critique results.

A successful way to handle stress and reduce anxiety is to challenge negative and distorted self-talk. Again, it is this private talk which defines who we are and what we can and cannot do. The goal is to adjust internal dialogue with external reality, to be aware of negative and distorted self-talk, and to ask ourselves, "What is the evidence for my conclusions?"

Albert Ellis (1958, 1962, 1976, 1979) and others have provided tactics for monitoring and changing negative self-talk.

This approach, called "Rational Therapy," is widely used in professional counseling and psychotherapy. The purpose of this tactic is to change negative and dysfunctional self-talk to more rational and positive inner conversations. This requires that we become aware of self-talk and challenge those hushed voices that are self-defeating. When our thinking is dominated by irrationality, irrational things happen to us. *It is not as important to speak to ourselves with affirming words as it is to recognize and challenge faulty, irrational, counter-productive self-talk.*

FROM SELF TO OTHERS

Throughout this chapter there has been an implicit subtext that is crucial to the development of the Invitational Leader — namely, how we think about ourselves and how we talk to ourselves have a profound impact on how we interact with others. Look, for example, at the words of the doctoral student in the previous section, and notice how his description of internal dialogue pertains exclusively to his conversations with other people. He says, "I talk out arguments with myself before I present them to other people," and "I often 'play out' difficult situations to better understand what went on in the interaction." Much of his internal dialogue, then, occurs either in preparation for a conversation with a colleague or in reflection upon a conversation that has already taken place. Again, how we talk with ourselves — and even *what we talk about* when we talk with ourselves — often is a means of mediating our social interactions.

If Invitational Leaders are those who enroll others in positive ways for beneficial activities, it follows that self-concept should be considered a vital aspect of their leadership. The intentionally inviting leader, one who is guided by a healthy, optimistic self-concept, frees others to feel as positively about themselves as he or she does. Further, because such a leader will have learned to be closely attuned to the dynamics of individual perceptions, he or she will be able to see things from the point of view of associates, encouraging them to develop similarly optimistic self-concepts. After all, how we interact with others is really a reflection of how we interact with ourselves. The Invitational Leader speaks in encouraging, positive tones, echoing what he hears when he listens carefully to his or her own whispering self.

It should come as no surprise that *listening* to ourselves and others is one of the keys to developing a healthy self-concept, for listening is vitally important to Invitational Leadership. Just as listening to the self helps us to monitor our self-talk for negative or unhealthy whispers, so listening closely to our colleagues enables us to understand differences in thinking styles and personalities. These are not always separate actions — listening to the self and listening to others — for they often happen simultaneously. One listens to the whispering self in determining how best to approach each colleague, and then monitors the interaction as it takes place, seeking to be as constructive and encouraging as possible.

It should be clear by now that the Invitational Leader's self-concept is crucial. Think, for instance, what would happen to the leader with a negative self-concept. How can negative thoughts about the self do anything but interfere with our relationships with others? How can the leader learn to engage others if he or she does not first learn to engage in confident and healthy self-talk? Further, what good is positive self-talk if the Invitational Leader does not treat colleagues and their opinions with respect? Consider what Robert Greenleaf (1996), an authority on the topic of servant leadership, writes about respectful listening:

> Most of us, at one time or another, some of us a good deal of the time, would *really* like to communicate, *really* get through to the level of meaning rooted in the listener's experience. It can be terribly impor-

tant. The best test of whether we are communicating at this depth is to ask ourselves, first, are we really *listening*? Are we listening to the one we want to communicate to? Is our basic attitude, as we approach the confrontation, one of wanting to understand? Remember that great line from the prayer of Saint Francis: "Lord, grant that I may not seek so much to be understood as to understand." (p. 305)

Understanding begins with the self—are we able to comprehend our own motivations and desires, and can we recognize and revise negative internal dialogue?—but such self-knowledge has broader implications for the ways in which we relate to others. Indeed, if we are "really listening" to ourselves, then we should be able to listen with equal concentration, respect, and interest to our colleagues. Heresy though it might be to do so, we might alter the prayer of Saint Francis: "Lord, grant that I may truly understand myself, and therefore learn to understand others."

A posture of seeking to understand ourselves and our place in the world is the stance of the Invitational Leader. The stakes of such understanding are high. We turn again to Greenleaf (1996): "I submit, with respect to purpose, that no person is to be trusted with any aim unless he or she has some contact, however tenuous, with ultimate purpose" (p. 94). The Invitational Leader has contact with his or her ultimate purpose of being a beneficial presence. This requires the soul-searching necessary to lead others toward greatness. More importantly, this leader will seek to inspire the same kind of search for meaning in his or her colleagues and, by setting a positive example through words and actions, will have a very real possibility of succeeding. At the highest level, then, the stakes of Invitational Education are nothing less than what Walt Whitman calls the "progress of souls."

CHAPTER THREE:
LEVELS OF FUNCTIONING:
OPENING DOORS TO SUCCESS

You can learn to lead, but don't confuse leadership with position and place. Don't confuse leadership with skills and systems or with tools and techniques. They are not what earn you the respect and commitment of your constituents. What earns you their respect in the end is whether you are you. And whether what you are embodies what they want to become. So just who are you, anyway?

James M. Kouzes, "Finding your Leadership Voice," *Leader to Leader*
(1999, p. 42)

In his essay "Finding Your Leadership Voice," James M. Kouzes (1999) writes that "aspiring leaders" must go through "a period of intense exploration—a period of going beyond technique, beyond training, beyond copying what the masters do" to discover that "there emerges from all those abstract strokes on the canvas an expression of self that is truly your own" (p. 42). In discussing self-concept theory and the "whispering self" in the previous chapter, we were really discussing this process of "intense exploration" as the leader first turns inward to develop positive internal dialogue. Yet the Invitational Leader cannot stop there. While discovering an

51

"expression of self that is truly your own" — identifying your ultimate purpose and meaning—is a lifelong process, so is the crucial work of encouraging your colleagues to perform their own explorations and make their own discoveries. Invitational Leadership is a collaborative journey, and it requires a leader who is able to turn with a generous spirit toward others so that he or she can listen, understand, and inspire.

We recognize that even the most committed Invitational Leader cannot sustain this generosity during every encounter and at every moment. However, he or she can strive for the level of functioning that most often embodies his or her best instincts. Gradually, the behavior that results will come to define his or her leadership.

There are four levels of functioning in Invitationl Leadership which include both helpful and harmful actions. Before they are presented, it may be useful to reflect on the "perceptual tradition" described in Chapter two. To some degree, levels of functioning are influenced by perceptions of the people involved. What might be judged as one level by some people might be judged as another level by others. An example might be helpful.

During World War II, General George S. Patton was invited to the Sultan of Morocco's palace in Casablanca. This invitation is considered by Arabs to be a great honor. General Patton immediately accepted, and asked if he might bring General Mark W. Clark, Commanding General, as well. A little later, the Sultan's Protocol called and said that General Clark should not come. General Patton became very much upset and offered not to go himself, but General Clark insisted that he go. This was very fortunate. General Patton soon discovered that the reason the Sultan did not want General Clark to attend was that he felt that he was of too high a rank to be invited so casually. Sometimes, what first appears to be disinviting might be an invitation in disguise.

Being human, all leaders function at each level from time to time, but it is the leader's *typical* level of functioning that determines his or her degree of commitment to the principles of Invitational Leadership. The levels are (1) intentionally disinviting, (2) unintentionally disinviting, (3) unintentionally inviting, and (4) intentionally inviting.

LEVEL ONE: INTENTIONALLY DISINVITING: THE DOOR IS SLAMMED SHUT

The most toxic and lethal level of leadership involves those actions, places, policies, programs, and processes that are deliberately designed to discourage, demean, or destroy. Indications of this level of functioning might be an administrator who publicly humiliates an associate, a company policy that is intentionally discriminatory, a prison program willfully designed to demean inmates, a "boot camp" for delinquent youth, or a school environment that is made deliberately unpleasant to "keep students in line." An example of this is a program called "assertive discipline." With this program, teachers are required to place the names of unruly students on the blackboard. Such practices as embarrassment and ridicule have no place in Invitational Leadership.

Unfortunately, some administrators resemble Elmira Gulch in the 1939 film version of L. F. Baum's *Wizard of Oz*. Like Elmira, they take pleasure in hurting people or seeing them upset. As one administrator bragged: "I don't have ulcers, I give them!" In our opinion, leaders who function at the intentionally disinviting level might benefit from seeking other employment or obtaining professional counseling. Their deliberate negative signals may be understandable, and even forgivable, but not justifiable. In Invitational Leadership, disinviting people, places, policies, programs, and processes cannot be justified regardless of effectiveness or efficiency. There is no justification for Invitational Leaders to remain at the intentionally disinviting level.

A graphic example of intentionally disinviting behavior

was shared by one of our graduate students:

> I have always remembered something which
> occurred in high school. At that time I was captain
> of a forensics group which often took out-of-town
> trips and thus had to stay overnight away from home,
> usually in a hotel. On this particular trip the super-
> vising teacher brought along a girl who helped her at
> school with secretarial work to act as her secretary at
> the forensics tournament. The girl was not especial-
> ly attractive and did not come from the social group
> which normally made up this forensics team. That
> night most of us gathered in one of the hotel rooms
> for talk, lots of laughter and winding down after the
> day's activities. This girl came and knocked on the
> door wanting to join our fun. (This was a time when
> fun was only talk.) But none of us would let the girl
> into the room. We got very quiet and pretended that
> no one was there. And I went along with this cruel-
> ty. The girl may not have known what was happen-
> ing, or if she did, I hope she has forgiven us. In any
> case, I still remember what happened, and I am still
> ashamed of my behavior.

Cruelty may be understandable in the context of what led to it;
therefore, it may perhaps be forgivable, but it is never justifiable.

Those who function at the intentionally disinviting level
deliberately create and maintain places, programs, policies, and
processes that are designed to inform people that they are incapable, worthless, and irresponsible. Adding insult to injury,
their intentionally disinviting behavior has direction, purpose,
and goals.

To us it is sad to note that there are those who take a certain joy in functioning at the level of contempt, distrust, and
pessimism. It may be because they see disinviting behavior as

a virtue in leadership. There are books on leadership that use Machiavelli, sharks, and even chain saws as their role models. It may also be because they function from a defensive, protective, and suspicious stance. They seek to lead through manipulation, deceit, and raw power. But regardless of reasons, such models do not fit with Invitational Leadership. This intentionally disinviting bottom level may be thought of as lethal functioning.

Lethal functioning occurs in at least two ways. The first happens when even the most skilled leader becomes angry and frustrated and makes a decision based on these feelings. Examples might be a judge who orders juvenile offenders to be locked up with hardened criminals to "teach them a lesson," a father who loses his temper and strikes his child, or an administrator who publicly berates a secretary. There is a great danger in the willingness of some leaders to legitimize intentionally disinviting actions.

While intentionally disinviting behavior is to be assiduously avoided, there are some rare circumstances where such behavior can be humorous. An example is an exchange of messages between Cornelius Vanderbilt and George Westinghouse in 1872. Westinghouse contacted Vanderbilt and asked him to listen to his idea for inventing an air brake. The crusty old President of the New York Central Railroad replied: "I have no time to waste on fools." Later, after the Pennsylvania Railroad successfully tested the brake, Vanderbilt summoned Westinghouse to see him. The inventor replied: "I have no time to waste on fools." When we say something that is intentionally disinviting, we may be giving the best speech we'll ever live to regret!

A second way that lethal functioning occurs is when leaders use their positions of power to behave unethically, illegally, or immorally. Examples of this might be the manager who attempts to seduce an employee, the prejudiced school counselor who repeatedly discourages certain students to apply for college, the attorney who misrepresents a client, or the company president who seeks to destroy a competitor through unfair practices.

A classic example of lethal functioning may be seen in the play Amadeus. It is Salieri, consumed by professional jealousy, who sets out with murderous intent to destroy Mozart. Salieri discovered Mozart's greatest fear, and used this knowledge with deadly effect. It is sad to note that there are some people who have a certain lethal talent for sending intentionally disinviting messages to others regarding their lack of value, abilities, or competencies.

A further example of lethal functioning was shared by one of our friends, a female principal, who decided to go back to school and earn her Ph.D. When she approached the university faculty advisor and expressed her desire to enroll in the doctoral program she was told to forget the idea, that she was not "marketable." At a meeting some weeks later she shared what had transpired with two of her female colleagues. The two women principals told her that they, too, had the desire to earn a doctorate and had talked with this same faculty advisor. They had also been discouraged from entering a doctoral program. As they talked, a male principal joined the conversation. He said that he had met with the same professor, and that he had been *encouraged* to enroll. It appears that this faculty advisor was a serial killer of female aspirations.

It is clear from this example that it is not always those leaders with the most authority who do the most damage to an organization. Indeed, those individuals in supervisory middle management roles can have a severely negative impact on an entire system. The female principal in the previous example will forever link her experience with the faculty advisor with her sense of the university itself. As she talks with other people about her experience, the university may slowly begin to acquire a reputation for gender discrimination.

No matter how inviting and encouraging the university's president might be, the actions of one faculty member have the potential to undermine much good and productive work. In large organizations, these situations inevitably arise, but still the Invitational Leader must be vigilant while attempting to create an inviting institution. Being human, leaders may slip into disinviting modes of functioning on occasion. We are, after all, human beings first and leaders second. Thankfully, most leaders who function at a disinviting level do so unintentionally, which brings us to the second level of functioning.

LEVEL TWO: UNINTENTIONALLY DISINVITING: THE DOOR IS LEFT CLOSED BY MISTAKE

Unintentionally disinviting people, places, policies, programs, and processes may be defined as forces in the environment that are functioning in negative and counter-productive ways even though leaders are unaware that this is taking place. When leaders create places, policies, programs, and processes that are unintentionally disinviting, they find themselves repeatedly asking questions like these:

> Why are we having so many employee turnovers?
> Why are employees not following our policies?
> Why are we losing customers?
> Why is morale so low?
> Why can't we get along better?
> Why are customers not showing up?
> Why are people so upset?

Leaders who function at the unintentionally disinviting level are usually well-meaning, but the behaviors they exhibit, the places they create, and the policies and programs they design and maintain are often uncaring, chauvinistic, condescending, patronizing, sexist, racist, homophobic, dictatorial, or just plain thoughtless. A colleague referred to this second level as "unconscious incompetence."

Examples of unintentionally disinviting behaviors

appear again and again when individuals describe incidents. An older adult complained that her pastor always shouted in her presence as though she were hard of hearing. A young employee expressed concern that his female boss referred to him as "Hunk." One woman commented: "I feel insulted when the director always asks a female to take minutes." Although unintended, such actions can be viewed by others as disinviting. It is a little like being hit by a truck; whether intentional or not, it still causes damage.

A disturbing example of unintentionally disinviting behavior was provided by the behavior of a surgeon. She completed a successful operation, but was so anxious to make her tee-time for a golf game that she left the hospital without taking time to speak to the patient's loved ones. They were left in the waiting room greatly concerned about the operation's outcome. Such forgetfulness can have costly consequences. Patients and their loved ones are far more likely to sue physicians and hospitals when they feel they have been treated badly.

Unintentionally disinviting processes can also be directed at oneself, as we described in Chapter Two. The whispering self of some individuals is constantly negative. They refer to themselves, both inwardly and outwardly, in such demeaning ways that if anyone else said such things they would be highly insulted. The damage caused by such thinking was beautifully described by Alexander Dumas (1844/1962):

> A person who doubts himself is like a man who
> would enlist in the ranks of his enemies and bear arms
> against himself. He makes his failure certain by him-
> self being the first person to be convinced of it.

Some people are totally unaware that that they are joining the ranks of their own enemies. In fact, they are being unintentionally disinviting to themselves.

Countless factors and variables influence the leader's daily activities. Interruptions from important work, pressures to attend meetings and complete tasks, demands from supervisors, over-due projects, personnel conflicts, physical ailments, noise level, even the temperature, weather, or time of day, week, or month—can influence both the degree of intentionality and level of functioning. At such times these myriad demands and factors can be such that leaders act or react in ways that are perceived by others as disinviting, even though this was not intended.

Illustrations of unintentionally disinviting behaviors are continuing to work at one's desk while someone stands there waiting to be recognized, drinking coffee during an interview without offering the interviewee a cup, giving a finger–crunching handshake, telling inappropriate jokes, answering the phone in a middle of a conversation, or even arranging office furniture so that the leader has a "throne" while visitors are seated in small, straight-back chairs

A typical example of unintentionally disinviting activity would be to decorate one's office with so many personal items (sail boats, cross-stitching, Zulu shields, dozens of family photos, athletic trophies, various collections of whatever) that visitors feel that they have blundered into someone's family room. Sometimes these actions and activities are caused by misdirected attempts to impress visitors with one's accomplishments. However, the most likely cause is a simple lack of sensitivity, politeness, and good manners. For this reason, civility, common courtesies, and sensitivity to appearance are given high priority in Invitational Leadership. Life is never so hurried or busy that the leader has no time for civility, politeness, and common courtesy.

Sometimes, attempts at humor can be unintentionally disinviting. What is meant to be funny can come across as mocking and even cruel. Consider these comments posted to office walls or placed on desks:

> "You have obviously mistaken me for someone who cares."

"Have a nice day, somewhere else."

"What part of NO don't you understand?"

"The next time you're passing by, keep going."

"Come on in, everything else has gone wrong today."

"I'd like to help you out, which way did you come in?"

While usually well-intentioned and meant to be funny, comments like the above can be unintentionally disinviting.

The importance of good manners was emphasized in early Japan, where young men were selected and trained to be Samurai Warriors. To illustrate, here is advice from the *Book of the Samuria*:

> When an official place is very busy and someone comes in thoughtlessly with some business or other, often there are people who will treat him coldly and become angry. This is not good at all. At such times, the etiquette of the Samurai is to calm himself and deal with the person in a good manner. (Tsunetomo, 1979, p. 37)

On some occasions, leaders send messages that in and of themselves would be viewed by most fair-minded observers as inviting. However, because individual perceptions play such an important role, the person who receives these messages may view them as disinviting. A classic example of unintentionally disinviting behavior was provided by the comic strip *Peanuts*.

One of the most popular strips that Charles Schultz (1968) ever drew is one in which the kids are looking at cloud formations, and Linus says: "That cloud up there looks a little like the profile of Thomas Eakins, the famous painter. And those up there look to me like the map of British Honduras. And that group over there gives me the impression of the stoning of Stephen... I can see the Apostle Paul standing there to one side." Then Lucy says, "Uh-huh. That's very good. What do YOU see in the clouds, Charlie Brown?" And Charlie says,

"Well, I was going to say I saw a ducky and a horsie, but I changed my mind." Shultz was able to bring back our almost forgotten memories of disinviting childhood experiences.

For Invitational Leaders to develop and maintain productive relationships with associates, it is vital that they nurture their ability to take an "internal" frame of reference: to view individuals as they see themselves, others, and the world. When it does happen that leaders are viewed as disinviting, it may be because their behaviors are careless, inappropriate, or both.

CARELESS BEHAVIOR

Sometimes leaders appear to be blissfully unaware of what others would like in terms of direction and support. Many colleges, for example, suffer a huge dropout rate. At some community colleges the attrition rate is over 50 percent during the first year. This dropout rate may be caused by the careless behavior of some college representatives who fail to provide appropriate academic advisement for students. It might also be exacerbated by failure to provide directional signs, adequate lighting, or convenient parking for students and visitors, while the best parking is reserved for faculty and staff. It is further exacerbated by poorly trained advisors who don't know what they're doing and who seemingly don't care.

Many people who visit community colleges and other institutions of higher learning for admissions information never follow through. One reason may be that they encounter careless advisors. Consider the following verbal directive given to a prospective student: "To enroll, go to the Registrars Office in Mossman Building, Room 265, pick up admissions forms A194 and B286. Complete both forms and turn them in, along with your fee schedule check and personnel survey, at the Business Office, Curry Building, Room 29." Such directions could be overwhelming and very disinviting to prospective students.

The prospective student's whispering self mutters: "This college is no place for me." As James Thomson wrote back in 1730:

> Oft, what seems
> A trifle, a mere nothing, by itself
> In some nice situations, turns the scale
> Of fate, and rules the most important actions.

Leaders who think invitationally understand that even the smallest negative factor can have a tremendous impact. As Gladwell (2000) pointed out in *The Tipping Point: How Little Things Can Make a Big Difference*, people are a lot more sensitive to their environments than they may seem. They are influenced by circumstances, conditions, and particulars of the physical and psychological environments in which they operate

Invitational Leaders work to create an environment that matches the spirit of the organization, remaining aware that physical space has a direct impact on psychological responses. This is especially true for organizations like educational institutions, hospitals, non-profits, and businesses that provide services to the general public. Not only are these organizations having to care for the welfare of employees, but they are also responsible to paying customers—and, in the case of hospitals, to patients in often dire circumstances. Any carelessness in these settings can have a profoundly negative impact on the public's perceptions of the overall organization—and again, in the case of hospitals, carelessness can mean the difference between life and death.

INAPPROPRIATE BEHAVIOR

Caring leaders can mean well, but through lack of experience or errors in judgments, they may behave in ways that are inappropriate to the situation. Examples of inappropriate behavior includ being over-friendly (smiling continuously), over-familiar (patting, hugging), and even over-bearing (not listening to what others are saying).

An incident that illustrates inappropriate behavior happened to one of the authors when he was invited to give the keynote at a large convention:

> Following the keynote address, all the participants headed for small-group workshops. I approached the conference registration area and asked the person behind the desk where I might get a cup of coffee. The person responded by asking abruptly: "What workshop are you with?" I explained that I was not with a workshop, to which the person responded: "Coffee is served at 10:30 am, you'll have to wait." At that moment a custodian walked by and said to me: "There's a coffee shop on the second floor, and I'm going that way. I'll show you where it is." The custodian was demonstrating caring and appropriate behavior, which cannot be said of the person behind the desk who was, at best, unintentionally disinviting.

As with careless behavior, inappropriate behavior can have an especially negative impact upon organizations that provide services to the public. For instance, it is hard to imagine a worse setting for inappropriate behavior than in a hospital. One of the authors experienced such inappropriate behavior upon taking her mother for an X-ray during a bout with pancreatitis:

> As soon as my mother was wheeled into the X-ray room, the nurse asked, without so much as looking at her, "Is Lentz here?" My mother replied, "Lentz?" I'm Vera Lentz," letting the nurse know that she is defined by more than her last name. Once the technician had finished the X-ray, he too, exhibited inap-

propriate behavior—and not a little impatience—on calling out, "Next!" There was no sign of concern for my mother, no sense of the situation's seriousness, and seemingly no interest whatsoever in a family's fear that the problem might be cancer rather than pancreatitis.

As the story continues, notice how easy it is to choose to behave appropriately. Notice, too, the results of such behavior:

The next day my mother and I returned for another round of X-rays, and both of us were pleasantly surprised by the inviting behavior of the nurse and technician now on duty. The nurse, upon seeing my mother enter the room, asked, "Are you Mrs. Vera Lentz?" She replied, "Yes, I'm Vera. Sometimes they call me Vivi." Already a personal, human connection had been established between my mother and the X-ray staff. As we waited for my mother's turn, the technician reassured my mother with these words: "It's cold in here, Mrs. Lentz. I'm going to let your daughter put her sweater over you while you wait." Finally, as we left the X-ray room, the technician again offered encouraging words: "Mrs. Lentz, I hope everything goes well for you. And I think it will, because you look well."

This visit was an altogether different experience than the one just twenty-four hours earlier. Both my mother and I were put at ease on the second visit, not only by the inviting demeanor of the nurse and technician, but also by their encouraging words and tone. The message was clear: we are human beings here, and we understand what you are going through. Clearly this was an invitational stance, one my mother responded to with a perfect parting line for

the technician, delivered in a loud stage whisper as
we left the room: " I *like* that one!"

Like those at the intentionally disinviting bottom level,
leaders who function at the unintentionally disinviting level
may experience positive results from time to time. This is not
too surprising. People are helped in all sorts of ways, sometimes in spite of the leadership provided. As the fictional detec-
tive Charlie Chan noted: "Strange events permit themselves the
luxury of occurring." However, when positive results occur
regularly, it is a good bet that the leader is functioning at an
inviting level, either unintentionally or intentionally.

LEVEL THREE: UNINTENTIONALLY INVITING: THE DOOR IS OPEN BUT CHAINED

Many leaders who function at the unintentionally inviting level have the personal qualities that contribute to successful leadership. They are sometimes referred to as "natural-
born" leaders. They are usually optimistic, respectful, and
trusting. *Yet the one critical quality they lack is intentionality.*
When one manager was exposed to Invitational Leadership, he
exclaimed, "Hell, I've been doing this for years, but I didn't
know what I was doing." Because some leaders lack intentionality, they are likely to be inconsistent in their work and unpredictable in their actions. The lack of consistency jeopardizes
their ability to lead.

Leaders who function at the unintentionally inviting
level resemble the early "barn-storming" airplane pilots. These
pioneer aviators did not know much about aerodynamics,
weather patterns, or global navigation systems. As long as they
stayed close to the ground, where they could follow railway
lines or highways, and the weather was favorable, they did
fine. But when night fell or the weather turned dangerous they
could easily become disoriented and lost. In challenging situa-

tions they lacked consistency in direction. Attempting to practice Invitational Leadership without an explicit theoretical rationale is like flying a plane without a map, preparing dinner without a plan, or driving at night without headlights.

The basic problem with functioning at the unintentionally inviting level is that the leader can become disoriented and unable to identify the reasons for his or her successes or failures. If whatever "it" is should stop working, the leader does not know how to start it up again or what changes to make. (In baseball this is known as a "slump.") In these situations the leader lacks a consistent stance—a dependable position from which to operate. A colleague, Charlie Branch, commented that he would rather work for a leader who is functioning at the intentionally disinviting level than for one who is unintentionally inviting. As Charlie explained: "At least with intentionally disinviting leaders you know where you stand; with unintentionally inviting leaders you never know." When the leader is unintentionally inviting, his or her credibility is at risk, for he or she depends too often on serendipitous leadership.

SERENDIPITOUS LEADERSHIP

The word *serendipity* comes from an old Persian folk tale describing the antics of the three Princes of Serendip. Although they were shrewd and discerning, they relied on chance. Because leaders who typically function at the unintentionally inviting level have personal qualities and strengths that are conducive to successful leadership, they are often considered capable. They know *what* they are doing, but not *why*. This lack of understanding is a serious barrier to their potential as leaders. It also places followers at risk, since the leader's approach is trial and error. The leader's success is not a product of intentionality, but rather a matter of serendipity or—to put it bluntly — pure chance.

Leaders who function at the uintentionally inviting level

are like amateurs who enjoy looking for Indian arrowheads. They know what to look for, and they may discover an arrowhead or two, but their luck is no match for the professional archaeologist who knows where, when, how, and what to look for in seeking relics. The archaeologist of Invitational Leadership is the one who knows when, where, how, and why to be intentionally inviting with oneself and others, personally and professionally, which brings us to the top level of functioning in Invitational Leadership.

LEVEL FOUR: INTENTIONALLY INVITING: THE DOOR IS OPENED WIDE

Intentionality allows Invitational Leaders to achieve direction, purpose, and skill in their actions. It is through intentionality that they are able to choose appropriate and caring strategies and to behave accordingly. In rough waters the leader who is functioning at the intentionally inviting level is consistent in direction and stays on course. By analogy, leaders who function at the intentionally inviting level are like command pilots of large jet airliners. Thanks to their specialized knowledge they can "fly on instruments" around and over dangerous weather fronts. This ability to chart and maintain a dependable flight pattern spells the difference between their success and failure in reaching their destinations in a safe and desirable manner.

The ability to maintain a consistent and desirable stance is important in both personal and professional functioning. Consistency moves the leader beyond the reality of technological proficiency toward a quality of character based as much on who he or she is as on what he or she knows. Invitational Leaders are living examples of their guiding principles. By serving as facilitators, barrier busters, and visionaries, they demonstrate desirable behavior.

It should be noted again that being intentionally inviting

requires a certain measure of courage and bravery. By definition, a leader is one who takes risks and breaks new ground. Without the courage to act, the leader becomes simply a participant or functionary, providing service but little or no inspiration. Leaders who have reached the intentionally inviting level have a special style, which is reflected in their ability to distinguish between factors that are visibly appropriate and those that are invisibly so.

VISIBLY APPROPRIATE FACTORS

Of all the behaviors exhibited by those who practice Invitational Leadership, the most noticeable are visible to the untrained eye. Visibly appropriate behavior and actions include clearly stated agendas and goals, precise speeches and memos, adequate formal and informal discussions and meetings, and specific e-mails, faxes, and other communicative processes. They may also include creating a wellness program for employees, introducing a fair and consistent promotion policy, placing cheerful posters and living green plants, sending cards, donating time to a retirement center, participating in a walk for charity, handling difficult situations in a caring and appropriate manner, giving an effective presentation, and handling responsibilities in an effective and timely manner.

Many colleges have established a visibly inviting approach to service by establishing a centrally located "Welcome Center" that is fully equipped with all necessary forms and staffed by knowledgeable and caring advisors who are on hand to assist prospective students with completing all necessary applications. They may often escort visitors to other offices as needed. This hospitality is followed up with phone calls to prospective students to insure that their questions were answered and needs addressed in a satisfactory manner. Such caring behaviors may be quickly forgotten by the college advisor, but they can have long-lasting positive effects on prospective students. As valuable as such processes are, an even more powerful part of Invitational Leadership is found in invisibly appropriate factors.

INVISIBLY APPROPRIATE FACTORS

The invisibly appropriate factors of Invitational Leadership consist of the leader's vision, values, hopes, aspirations, and beliefs. These inner processes are revealed through unobtrusive factors that do not call attention to themselves. Few people witness them, and only the trained eye of other Invitational Leaders can detect them. Still, they have a tremendous impact on the lives of human beings. A doctoral student described the process as "artlessly inviting." It is carried out with such skill and grace that the art itself is invisible to all but the trained observer. As the Fox explains in *The Little Prince*: "And now here is my secret, a very simple secret: It is only with the heart that one can see rightly; what is essential is invisible to the eye" (De Saint-Exupery, 1943).

Invitational Leadership does not consist of unbridled display of one's immediate emotions any more than skillful social behavior consists of rampant disclosure or unsparing authenticity. Invitational Leadership at times requires the curtailment of certain emotions and the display of feelings more appropriate to the immediate situation.

At its best, Invitational Leadership reveals itself as an art. To borrow from the writings of Chuang-tse, an ancient Chinese philosopher, it should "flow like water, reflect like a mirror, and respond like an echo." As in any art form, the process should not call attention to itself. As Ovid explained in the *Art of Love*, "*Ars est celare artem*" — that is, art lies in concealing art. George Burns, in describing his work as the "straight man" for his wife and comedienne partner, Gracie, said, "I improved so much I finally got so good that nobody knew I was there." According to Lao-Tse, a sixth-century philosopher, "A leader is best when people barely know he exists. Not so good when people obey and acclaim him. Worse when they despise him. But of a good leader who talks little, when his work is done, his aim fulfilled, they will say 'We did it ourselves.'" In its purest form, Invitational Leadership remains unseen, and the art of being artless is mastered.

As an illustration of the invisibility of art, consider an audience observing the accomplished musician, the headline comedian, the world-class athlete, the Oscar-winning actor, or the master teacher. What these artists do seems effortless. Only when we try to duplicate the artistry do we realize that true art requires painstaking effort, personal discipline, and an enormous amount of intentionality. Three examples from the world of entertainment illustrate the value of being "artlessly inviting."

By all accounts, W. C. Fields was one of the greatest jugglers who ever lived. But technical skill was not enough for him. He transcended technique and perfected the genius of the intentional error. In the middle of a difficult feat, Fields would deliberately drop an object, apparently by accident. Then he would catch it in a second, also apparently accidental, move.

A second example of the perfection of art was provided by Ginger Rogers, the beautiful Hollywood actress and dancer, in describing dancing with the incomparable Fred Astaire. "It's a lot of hard work, that I do know," said Rogers. "But it doesn't look it, Ginger," someone responded. Replied Rogers, "That's why it's magic."

The third example comes from the ranks of the great comedy teams of the first half of the twentieth century. In those days the "straight man" was often more highly regarded than the more visible comic. Steve Allen explained that the straight man generally received top billing—for example, "Abbott and Costello," "Burns and Allen," and "Martin and Lewis." According to Allen, "It is no longer recognized how difficult 'playing straight' really is. Ultimately, the very ease of Abbott's talent makes it difficult for many to see how really good he was." To paraphrase Alexander Pope, true ease in leadership comes from art, not chance, as those move easiest who have learned to dance.

The highest level of professional functioning has many names. World-class athletes call it finding the "zone." Fighter pilots refer to "rhythm." Comedians speak of finding the "center." Football teams call it "momentum." Martial arts experts call it "sparkle." Religious leaders speak of "a state of grace." Here is how James Joyce (1916/1964) described this artistry:

> The artist, like the God of the creation, remains within or behind or beyond or above his handiwork, invisible, refined out of existence, indifferent, paring his fingernails. (p. 215)

But by whatever name this indefinable chemistry is called, it is possible to become so fluent, with one's principles and techniques so honed and combined, that an indefinable power is created—a force, tempo, synchronicity—and the presence and influence of Invitational Leadership becomes invisible to the untrained eye. A recent term for this high level of functioning has been described by M. Csikszentmihalyi (1990) as "flow." Flow is the holistic sensation that we sometimes feel when we are completely immersed in an activity where challenge and ability match.

Rather than using Csikszentmihalyi's beautiful word "flow," we like to say that an Invitational Leader functioning at the invisibly inviting level is truly "inspirited." This word suggests that the best leaders are *animated* by an indefinable source within themselves that literally gives them the breath of life, as the word denotes. It is for this reason that practice alone will never make one into an Invitational Leader. As James Kouzes (1999) writes in the epigraph with which we began this chapter, "Don't confuse leadership with skills and systems or with tools and techniques." An inspirited leader requires a formidable set of skills and tools, certainly, but he or she also requires a developed self that makes possible the optimal exercise of these skills and methods.

In short, this means that the Invitational Leader will have performed the intentional and intense process of self-exploration recounted in the previous chapter. He or she will have tapped into his or her authentic self, having studied closely the many varieties of leadership and having undergone a period of careful self-reflection. He or she will have emerged from this process a much wiser, more grounded, and more inviting person. Again, as Kouzes writes, "What earns you ... respect in the end is whether you are you." Invitational Leadership, then, is ideally an expression of the inspirited personality — one's authentic self — especially as it is revealed in the act of inviting. How this is done — *the practice of Invitational Leadership* — will occupy the remainder of our book.

PART II

The Practice

Part one of our book introduced the four principles of Invitational Leadership (respect, trust, optimism, and intentionality), the three foundations (perceptual tradition, self-concept theory, and the whispering self), and the four levels of functioning (intentionally disinviting, unintentionally disinviting, unintentionally inviting, intentionally inviting). It explained how these principles, foundations, and levels combine to establish the context of Invitational Leadership.

Part two of our book connects these principles, foundations, and levels to the process of becoming an Invitational Leader. This involves the four dimensions of successful functioning: (1) inviting ourselves professionally, (2) inviting others professionally, (3) inviting ourselves personally, and (4) inviting others personally. We have named these the "four corner press" because they continuously compete for time and energy. This competition creates stress and pressure, as the following drawing illustrates:

Being professionally inviting with oneself	Being professionally inviting with others
Being personally inviting with oneself	Being personally inviting with others

The necessity of balancing the four dimensions was expressed by Gerald Johnson: "Surely there is no figure more truly pitiable than the man of high intelligence who has devoted that intelligence, exclusive of all else, to something that is bound to lose its flavor just about the time he reaches full maturity, and who finds at the very moment when he is prepared to enjoy the fruits of his long labor that he has mixed himself a drink that, however excellent, is flat and tasteless." Overemphasizing or neglecting any one of the four dimensions causes stress on the other three. All the success in the world in one dimension will not make up for lack of success in the others. To define ourselves in terms of only one dimension, while ignoring the other three, would be to commit a form of psychological suicide . . . killing off large parts of our very existence. In Invitational Leadership, the objective is to develop optimally in all four dimensions. Like a well-tuned engine, each cylinder or piston should be in harmony with all the others. The more completely we as Invitational Leaders can excel in balancing the four, the more likely we are to realize our own potential for fulfillment. We invite ourselves by inviting others to succeed.

This leads us to the inescapable conclusion that Invitational Leadership is the use of one's self in creative and healthy ways. Leaders who think invitationally seek to release the energy of their associates so that they use their capacities to their fullest extent. This will not happen unless the leader is alive to life. There is no greater barrier to inviting others than to be disinviting with oneself. Invitational Leadership cannot be understood if it is thought of as an isolated series of behaviors, skills, or techniques. Rather, becoming an Invitational Leader is an intentional internal process that determines how we invite ourselves and others, personally and professionally. As we have said before, what is essential in Invitational Leadership is not the skills we possess, the techniques we use, or the hours we spend working, but the way we intentionally live and balance our lives.

Stoll and Fink (1996) reported that almost all studies of

leadership have tended to consider the professional activities of leaders while neglecting the importance of and interactions between the personal and professional lives of leaders. We address this importance and these interactions in the next four chapters. Chapter four describes the process of inviting ourselves professionally. This includes continuous exploration, education, and efforts to manage challenging conflicts in an inviting manner. Chapter five considers the importance of inviting others professionally, and involves the "Five Powerful P's" that make up an organization. Our sixth chapter explains how we invite ourselves personally and considers such ways as emotionally, physically, intellectually, and semantically. Our seventh chapter concludes the four-corner press by examining how we invite others personally through respect, care, and the celebration of life. Chapter eight, the concluding chapter, ties everything together by identifying the Invitational Leader as servant.

Being a leader is demanding. Balancing the demands of our professional and personal lives can be a major challenge for those of us who have invested our lives in becoming leaders. It is tempting to become an over-expecter, always finding ways to enhance ourselves as leaders, even at the risk of losing out in other dimensions of life. Committing ourselves obsessively to one dimension, while ignoring other areas, is like being perched on a one-legged stool. At the moment of our greatest triumph we discover that our success has been purchased at too great a price. Invitational Leaders seek satisfaction and gratification in all healthy dimensions of life, including those of family, friends, colleagues, community, religion, hobbies, and play as well as work.

CHAPTER FOUR:
INVITING OURSELVES
PROFESSIONALLY

When Yen Ho was about to take up his duties as tutor to the heir of Ling Duke of Wei, he went to Ch'u Po Yo for advice. "I have to deal with a man of depraved and murderous disposition . . . How is one to deal with such a person?" Ch'u Po Yo replied: "I am glad you asked that question, Yen Ho. In order to improve the behavior of others, you must first improve yourself."
—Taoist story of ancient China (Bennis & Nanus, 1985)

Perhaps never before in human history has there been such a need for leaders to keep abreast of what is happening in the world. Technological advances, social changes, medical discoveries, and countless other fast-moving trends impact on our ability to lead. Indeed, information reaches us today at a staggering rate. It is estimated that by the year 2020 the information available to us will double every seventy-three days. Even the most efficient leader will find it impossible not to sink beneath this avalanche of facts, theories, and trivia. Added to this pressure to keep up is the equally troubling pressure to discern amid all this information that which is truly useful. Anyone who has casually surfed the internet, for example, will

77

quickly discover that any given search will produce an inordinate amount of junk — sites that are incomplete, impossible to navigate, infrequently updated, totally irrelevant, or just plain amateurish.

It is perhaps no coincidence that this phenomenal increase in information occurs at a time when America's work ethic seems to have taken on a new intensity. For a new generation of workers, many of whom are in the technology industry, it is not uncommon for work to become a nearly round-the-clock endeavor. The stresses, particular to this generation of workers, are different in kind from those that beset older generations. Older workers also face unusual pressures of their own in this technological age. The pressure to continue learning and exploring becomes even greater as these workers watch routine practices being transformed by sometimes intimidating technological advances. It seems the pace never slows, creating in workers of all ages what Richard Saul Wurman (1989) calls "information anxiety": "Information anxiety is produced by the ever-widening gap between what we understand and what we think we should understand" (p. 222). The more information bombards us, the less secure we become in our knowledge. Do we know enough? Do we work hard enough? The answer seems to be never.

Jeremy Rifkin, president of the Foundation of Economic Trends, presented a new term — 24/7 — which has entered the professional vocabulary. This describes our around-the-clock, twenty-four-hours-a-day, seven-days-per-week activity. Locked in with always-on-duty fax machines, e-mails, voice mails, PC's, Palm Pilots and cellular phones, 24-hour trading markets, ATMs, on-line banking services and e-commerce, there is virtually no escape. Combine all this with open-all-night restaurants, drugstores, twenty-four hour on-line trading and service centers, and clearly there is little rest for the weary.

While technology has dramatically increased the pace and flow of commercial and social activity, there seems to be less and less time for relaxation or even sleep. On airline flights, people entering and leaving the plane are shouting into their cellular phones, and they work feverishly at their lap tops the moment they are given permission by the flight attendants to turn them on. The unhappy result of all this frantic activity often appears in the name of "air rage," "road rage," and "office rage." More and more people are expressing their stress with violent outbursts.

Needless to say, these undue pressures can also lead to conflicts in the work place, as employees begin to feel less sure about both knowledge and performance. This situation puts leaders in a precarious position, as they too must keep the "blade bright" even as they offer their associates a vision of how to absorb these rapid changes and retain some sense of equilibrium. What this means is that it is necessary for Invitational Leaders to first learn to lessen their own "information anxiety" by taking responsibility for their own continuous education and exploration. They must also turn within to discover the most effective methods of managing relationships. In short, they are required to invite themselves professionally, beginning with continuous education.

CONTINUOUS EDUCATION

Like all other professionals, leaders pursue years of academic training to acquire and refine their beliefs, knowledge, and skills. Becoming an Invitational Leader is a marathon, not a sprint. It usually takes years to obtain knowledge, acquire a vision, and communicate that vision to associates. This requires continuing studies, re-calibrating vocabularies, updating skills, mastering new technologies, studying new research findings, and discovering fresh ways to improve professional functioning. It also may require enrolling in a college course, attending professional meetings and workshops, and presenting at local, state, regional, national, and international conferences.

As we have seen, the work of keeping up with new technologies in itself can become a full-time job, but clearly a leader must do far more than grasp the significance of the latest software. The new information age requires equally intense learning in more traditional areas. Think, for instance, of the fundamental questions about education raised by the presence of computers in the classroom. Think of the moral and ethical dilemmas posed by recent scientific and medical advances. Think about the philosophical questions that must be encountered by those on the forefront of space exploration. Or think generally about the wide range of issues that attend a world increasingly being driven by technology: What about those without access to technology? How much progress is too much? How do our traditional humanistic values fit into this brave new world?

For the Invitational Leader, questions about morality, ethics, and philosophy should never be very far away from any action. This is not to say that the Invitational Leader should be like Rodin's famous "Thinker," who is forever absorbed in tragic reflection. Rather, it means that the Invitational Leader's actions must be informed by an overarching vision, one born of careful grappling with the profound issues of the day. Lifelong learning, then, is really a continuous effort to live an examined life. As Robert Greenleaf (1996) reminds us, a person who has not considered his or her "ultimate purpose" should not be trusted to lead (p. 94).

So how do any of us make time for such learning, *in addition* to keeping abreast of the latest developments in our fields? First of all, we adopt a frame of mind conducive to continuous education, remaining open to fresh ideas and new subjects. Consider, for instance, what could be accomplished by devoting as little as fifteen to twenty minutes per day to new learning. Start on Monday with a brief exploration of suggested web sites. On Tuesday read the feature article on medical ethics in *The Atlantic Monthly*. Designate Wednesday as your poetry day and reread one of Keats's great odes. On Thursday review the annual reports of your top competitors. Read a chapter from the latest best-selling book on leadership on Friday. On Saturday catch up on the week's editorials in the *Wall Street Journal*, and on Sunday expand your 15-20 minutes by enjoying the *New York Times* over a leisurely breakfast.

Following this schedule, with variations for particular fields and interests, can have a profound impact on day-to-day living. Lessons can be gleaned from the most unlikely sources, and finding them requires that we remain curious and inquisitive. Above all, it requires that we invite ourselves professionally to continue learning. The Invitational Leader might lament with the poet: the life so short, the art so long to learn. By applying ourselves to continuous education with concentration and enthusiasm, however, we will spend less time lamenting how little we know, and much more quality time discovering the true pleasures of lifelong learning.

CONTINUOUS EXPLORATION

Continuous quest for understanding involves talking with colleagues about leadership, attending training institutes, and seeking new and innovative approaches to problem-solving. Albert Einstein called this continuous exploration a "holy curiosity." Everybody is going somewhere. Invitational Leaders choose to become more knowledgeable, more inspirited, and more passionate about their work.

As with continuous education, constant exploration in our fields begins when we invite ourselves professionally to embrace innovation and change. Invitational Leaders keep themselves open to changes in their professions and find in competition a healthy desire to reach a higher level of functioning. Another phrase for continuous exploration is *boundary monitoring*, the careful examination of what is happening at the leading edge of the profession. In business those at the leading edge are called benchmarkers, setting examples that are emulated by competitors. A leader can monitor the boundaries of his or her field by attending conferences, reading magazine articles, enjoying dinner meetings with associates and colleagues. The opportunity for this crucial work is everywhere, but the Invitational Leader must approach the boundaries with a kind of open curiosity. Approaching things in this way, he or she will soon find that fresh ideas come naturally and in rapid succession, and that inspiration is never very far away.

In their book *The Leadership Challenge*, Kouzes and Posner (1995) offer another useful term for boundary monitoring: *outsight*. If we think of continuous learning as a process of gaining deeper *in*-sight into oneself and one's ultimate purpose, then we might understand constant exploration as the achievement of *out*-sight:

> Outsight is the power of perceiving external realities
> . . . . Leaders must destroy confining barriers. Those
> who enclose themselves, who shut doors to the world
> outside, will never be able to detect change. And,
> worse, they may be overtaken by it. Over and over
> again, [leaders] we interviewed told us that [they]
> keep their eyes and ears open. They permit passage
> of new ideas into the system. (p. 59)

We might go one step further here and say that not only do leaders "permit" new ideas but they also consciously *seek them out*. Indeed, Invitational Leaders are willing above all to take chances, and to encourage similarly healthy risk-taking in their associates.

The leader who remains open to the possibility of change—who promotes change—also possesses a certain amount of what Kouzes and Posner call "psychological hardiness" (p. 67):

> People with a hardy attitude . . . take the stress of life
> in stride. When they encounter a stressful event—
> whether positive or negative—(1) they consider it
> interesting, (2) they feel that they can influence the
> outcome, (3) they see it as an opportunity for devel-
> opment. This optimistic appraisal of events increas-
> es their capacity to take decisive steps to alter the sit-
> uation. (p. 67)

We have already explored the importance for Invitational
Leaders of maintaining an optimistic and realistic self-concept.
Optimism tempered by reality breeds psychological hardiness,
and hardiness inspires associates to embrace, rather than fear,
change. The Invitational Leader can go a long way toward
reducing stress-related conflicts in the workplace by nurturing
an environment where change is associated with innovation and
positive development, and where boundary monitoring (or outsight) becomes a deeply interesting and fulfilling process of
professional exploration.

ACHIEVING BALANCE

As we work to realize our full potential as leaders, it is
possible to over-use our potentialities in one area at the expense
of the others. This is most likely to occur when we expect too
much of ourselves. Here is how Charles Swindoll (1983)
described the "over-expecter":

> To the over-expecter, enough is never enough. There
> is always room for improvement, always an area or
> two that isn't quite up to snuff, always something to
> criticize, always. The over-expecter uses words like
> "ought" and "should" and loves sentences that
> include "must" and "more." To them, "work harder"
> and "reach higher" are rules rather than exceptions.

> Fun fades, laughter leaves, and what remains? This
> won't surprise anyone: the tyranny of the urgent, the
> uptight, the essential, the expected. Always the
> expected. Which being interpreted, means, the mak-
> ing of a coronary. (p. 224)

When work is the dominant force in our lives it can lead to
tragedy. In the Japanese language "karoshi" means death from
overwork. The Japanese recognize karoshi as a legitimate
national malady that may be responsible for the deaths of thousands of workers a year in Japan. To avoid karoshi, it is vital
that we seek balance and harmony in relating to ourselves and
others, personally and professionally. Suzuki expressed this
balance and harmony beautifully: "I am an artist at work, and
my work of art is my life."

When we invite ourselves professionally, we pledge to
explore the great world outside our office door, as well as that
within our hearts and minds. Clearly there is an enormous personal component to the professional invitations we issue ourselves. Anne Morrow Lindbergh (1955) captures something of
that personal component in her book *Gift From the Sea*:

> I want first of all — in fact, as an end to these other
> desires — to be at peace with myself. I want a sin-
> gleness of eye, a purity of intention, a central core to
> my life that will enable me to carry out these obliga-
> tions and activities as well as I can. I want, in fact —
> to borrow from the language of the saints — to live
> in grace as much of the time as possible. I am not
> using this term in a strictly theological sense. By
> grace I mean an inner harmony. (p. 23)

The four qualities of Invitational Leadership (optimism,
trust, respect, and intentionality) serve as guiding principles to
achieve this inner harmony. Optimism is evidenced by the
leader's perceptions of present and future options. Trust reveals

itself in our acceptance of change, our willingness to take risks and find new ways to be. Respect is evidenced by positive and realistic internal dialogue regarding oneself, others, and the world. Intentionality is demonstrated by the Invitational Leader's direction and purpose in life.

CONTINUOUS EFFORTS TO MANAGE CONFLICTS

Of all the challenges that the Invitational Leader faces, perhaps the greatest is to be inviting to oneself professionally when others may be being disinviting. Yet a hallmark of Invitational Leadership is to be "inviting in the rain." Anyone can be inviting when the sun is shining and everything is going well. It requires continuous effort to manage conflicts with the least expenditure of energy, in the quickest amount of time, and with respect for oneself and others.

Conflicts are a normal aspect of human interactions. Crises are normal, problems arise, tensions are inevitable, and complications can be expected. Often these situations are opportunities for new ideas and fresh innovations. In some happy situations, they can be handled by letting them take care of themselves, without interference, as the following story from ancient China suggests:

> King Hsuan of Chou heard of Po Kung-i, who was reputed to be the strongest man in his kingdom. The King was dismayed when they met, since Po looked so weak. When the King asked Po how strong he was, Po said mildly, "I can break the leg of a spring grass-hopper and withstand the winds of an autumn cicada." Aghast, the King thundered, "I can tear rhinoceros leather and drag nine buffaloes by the tail, yet I am ashamed of my weaknesses. How can you be famous?" Po smiled and answered quietly, "My teacher was Tzu Shang-chiui, whose strength was

without peer in the world, but even his relatives
never knew it because he never used it."
(Anonymous)

An Invitational Leader may reasonably be held to a higher standard of behavior than associates. We are expected to behave in accordance with our stated principles, exercise a higher degree of restraint, have more compassion for the human foibles of associates, and accomplish goals through voluntary compliance, rather than coercion or brute force.

Conflict management, from the perspective of Invitational Leadership, requires that we apply the principles of respect, trust, optimism, and intentionality to the most difficult concerns, problems, and challenges. In our judgments, failure to apply these principles is among the major causes of conflict, both personal and professional.

At the heart of Invitational Leadership is personal control over the whispering self. This hushed inner voice should remind us that the great majority of people are well-meaning. Just because there may be a few individuals who might wish us ill does not mean that everyone is mischievous. Moreover, their disinviting behavior should not control what we do. According to the *Talmud*, when a wise man loses his temper, he is no longer wise.

The whispering self should remind us to apply the principles of Invitational Leadership in handling any problem or frustration at the lowest possible level, using the least amount of energy and time. The goal is to obtain maximum effectiveness with a minimum of effort. Decisions are made at the lowest possible level consistent with the principles of Invitational Leadership. A scene from the television program *Happy Days* illustrates how this works.

The "Fonz" was planning to spend Christmas alone in his tiny apartment. His friend Richie's father insisted that Fonzie spend Christmas at their home. Fonzie declined, and the father tried to *order* Fonzie to spend Christmas with them.

The Fonz bristles and says he's not going anywhere! About that time Fonzie's friend, Richie, stepped in and said: "Wait, Fonzie, you don't understand... it's an *invitation*, Fonzie, my Father is inviting you to be with us." The Fonz thought a moment, then replied, "Oh, well, if it's an *invitation*... in that case I accept." It is far easier to redirect and re-conceptualize, rather than out-tough, the Fonz. This concept of redirecting and re-conceptualizing, rather than out-toughing, is critical in becoming an Invitational Leader.

Marv Levy, a 2001 Professional Football Hall of Fame inductee, explained his coaching philosophy this way: "Leadership is the ability to get other people to get the best out of themselves. It is manifested by getting them not to follow you, but to join you." Working together with respect, trust, optimism, and intentionality is a hallmark of Invitational Leadership.

It will be helpful here to pause and reflect on the nature of an invitation. At first blush the term may conjure up a concept of weakness or softness, particularly when compared with such terms as "empower," "control," "master," "giving orders," and "taking charge." But be not misled. It takes courage and bravery to be inviting. Creating and maintaining organizations guided by the principles of respect, trust, optimism, and intentionality requires moral strength. Invitational Leaders face and deal with challenges that are difficult, unpleasant, and painful. Confronting rather than withdrawing from these challenges is essential to becoming an Invitational Leader. This is accomplished by shifting from control and command to connectedness, cooperation, and communication. The goal is to resolve, or at least manage, situations through non-coercive means

In any situation, major or minor, personal or professional, where there is the potential for problems or conflicts, the Invitational Leader's internal voice (the whispering self) should ask: "How can I manage this situation at the lowest possible level, using the least amount of energy, that is in keeping with the principles of Invitational Leadership?" Handling concerns in this way is in keeping with the "law of parsimony," which is a maxim that things should not be multiplied beyond necessity. This maxim is sometimes called "Occam's Razor" after William of Occam, a fourteenth-century philosopher. Occam's Razor maintains that the simplest explanation is always the best, provided it covers all the circumstances. Anyone can turn a situation into a major confrontation, but why cut a rope that can easily be untied?

The challenge for those of us as Invitational Leaders is to find the middle ground between protecting our own rights on the one hand without infringing on the rights of others on the other hand. To think invitationally does not mean to be blind to people who might wish us ill. Respecting our own rights without stepping on the rights of others is central. When leaders continually sacrifice their own rights to meet the demands of others, the sacrifice builds resentment in the leader and contempt for the leader among associates.

As explained by Alberti and Emmons (1990) in their book *Your Perfect Right: A Guide to Assertive Behavior*, we only hurt ourselves, and ultimately other people, when we have a fatal desire to please or to behave in such a way as to never disinvite anyone under any circumstances. When we sacrifice our rights, we summon others to take advantage of us.

The importance of asserting ourselves has been documented by Alberti and Emmons, who defined assertive behavior as those personal actions that enable us to act in our own best interests, to stand up for ourselves without undue anxiety, to express our honest feelings comfortably, and to exercise our own rights without denying the rights of others. Alberti and Emmons view assertive behavior as affirming our own rights (in contrast to aggressive behavior, which is directed against others), which, they say, is the "perfect right" of every individual.

Beyond affirming our own rights, assertive behavior also involves the ability to express our feelings of appreciation, positive regard, and affection. To illustrate, one of the authors was on a long overseas flight when a flight attendant came down the isle with a service cart. When she handed me a drink I noticed that her hands were beautiful. I took the liberty of expressing how attractive I thought her hands were. She looked at me and said: "You will never know how much I needed that compliment. Thank you." When appropriate and caring, Invitational Leaders take the risk of expressing appreciation for the beautiful things in life.

Advantages of assertive behavior have been documented by research. Seligman (1975, 1990), who formulated theories of learned helplessness and learned optimism, stated that the experience of internal control (a healthy whispering self) is essential to both positive self-esteem and good psychological health. The problem with learned helplessness is that when our whispering self murmurs that we lack control, this hushed voice persists even when circumstances have been altered and we actually have authority and power to act.

While assertiveness is healthy, the principles of Invitational Leadership (respect, trust, optimism, and intentionality) help to safeguard us from having our assertiveness become aggression. Being human, we are sometimes tempted to run rough-shod over people, particularly when we have the desire and power to do so. We have all known individuals who achieved a certain kind of success through intentionally disinviting practices. However, in the final analysis, these individuals usually pay a high price for denying the rights of others and ignoring their feelings.

A sad example of how one can get his or her "comeuppance" is provided by Albert Dunlap (1996), perhaps best remembered as "Chain Saw Al." Dunlap built his reputation on corporate heartlessness. His book, *Mean Business: How I Save Bad Companies and Made Good Companies Great,* glorified the virtues of firing large numbers of people to inflate the price of company stock. After initial successes, Dunlap found himself facing charges in a civil suit by the Securities and Exchange Commission. Moreover, Sunbeam's shares, which soared to $52.00 the day Dunlap was hired to head the company, fell to seven and a half cents after the SEC filed its charges. Those who accept Invitational Leadership as their model are a far cry from practicing mean business. Moreover, those who feel mistreated will become frustrated and hostile, which may later return as vengeance.

Two additional factors in this introduction to managing concerns is the critical importance of preventing problems whenever possible and keeping a sense of humor. Preventing problems requires a special talent based on simple survival. Here is how Phil Silvers, the great comedian, talked about survival:

> The road requires an extra talent—survival. Experienced troupers acquire the art of sniffing out catastrophe before it happens. You have to be able to change direction, improvise instantly. On tour, only one thing is certain: If it is impossible for the conductor to fall into the orchestra pit and break his leg—he will do it. (p. 188)

Through humor, according to Charles Chaplin, we see in what seems rational, the irrational; in what seems important, the unimportant. It also sharpens our sense of survival and preserves our sanity. Leaders who lack a sense of humor become dangerous to themselves and dangerous to others. Moreover, a good sense of humor can help us to counter personal irritations and everyday frustrations. It seems true that laughter is good for the soul.

To operate at the lowest level possible in managing conflicts, the Invitational Leader should employ the "Rule of the Six C's." The goal is to employ the lowest "C' first, then move upward toward higher C's only as absolutely necessary to resolve the situation. The six powerful C's are: "concern," "confer," "consult," "confront," "combat," and "conciliate."

CONCERN

In any situation or circumstance, major or minor, personal or professional, where there appears to be a problem or difficulty, the first step is to identify and define the concern. Once it has been clearly identified and defined, the second step is to ask: "Is this really a matter of concern?" It is not so much a matter of what happens to us, but how we interpret and react to what happens. Some concerns may be comfortably overlooked. Moreover, they may solve themselves without our interference.

For example, at the beginning of a meeting there may be numerous private conversations taking place among the participants. Rather than making an issue of trying to get the group to "quiet down" by shouting, the Invitational Leader allows the concern to resolve itself by beginning the meeting on time in a business-like manner and letting the agenda take over. In most cases participants will quickly settle down to the business at hand.

Two good ways to solve a concern are to discover that none exists, and to find that the concern is unsolvable. The old adage "Don't cry over spilt milk" means that what is done is done. Some concerns cannot be resolved. For example, as we grow old we face aging bones, brittle teeth, gray hair (or none at all!), and the loss of youthful energy. Father Time and Mother Nature are relentless. There are some concerns we just have to learn to live with as best we can, hopefully with good humor and grace.

The concern may be as minor as someone interrupting a meeting with small talk, placing luggage on an empty seat at a crowded airport, breaking in line at a theatre, or telling an off-color joke. It may also be a major concern, such as an illegal activity, unethical behavior, or unprofessional conduct. In some cases it may be as simple as a situation that causes us personal discomfort. For example, a colleague of one of the authors started calling him "Purkey The Turkey." This was a clear concern!

Here are some questions that the Invitational Leader might ask himself or herself to determine if a situation really is a concern:

1. Is it a concern because of my own biases, hang-ups, prejudices, or my need to impress associates with my power?
2. Are principles involved, such as legality, ethics, or morality?
3. Can this situation be overlooked without causing me personal stress?
4. Have I confined my concern only to one issue?
5. Am I being sufficiently flexible in this situation?
6. Is the other person in any shape to hear the concern, and if so, can he or she do anything about it?
7. Am I willing to accept the responsibility for bringing the concern up?
8. Do I know what I want to achieve in advance of conferring?
9. Do I have adequate information regarding my concern?

By asking the above questions of ourselves, we may find that the situation is not of sufficient concern that it justifies the time and effort needed to resolve it. What at first appears to be a concern may actually be a simple preference.

There are times, of course, when a situation is sufficiently troublesome that it requires more than analysis. It requires action. The key is not to wait too long. The concern should be expressed early and clearly so that it does not fester or escalate into an even larger and more troublesome situation. Should action be required, and once sufficient information and resources are available, it is time to confer.

CONFER

Conferring begins with calming ourselves down, even when the views of others are sharply different from ours. If we cannot control ourselves, we cannot control situations. As an ancient Chinese saying warns, "He who angers you controls you." We calm others down by our calmness.

Maintaining self-control in challenging situations or in the midst of provocations is a hallmark of Invitational Leadership. A classic example was provided by Sir Philip Sidney of eighteenth-century England. A foolish young man quarreled with him and tried to provoke him to fight by spitting in his face.

"Young man," said Sir Philip, "if I could as easily wipe blood from my conscience as I can wipe this insult from my face, I would this moment take your life." Leaders control their emotions; they do not let their emotions control them.

When expressing a concern, it is necessary to confine ourselves to one issue at a time. Otherwise, we may find ourselves dealing with several issues at once. Avoid counter-concerns until the original concern has been clearly expressed and acknowledged. Counter-concerns can be considered after the original concern has been addressed. This is not to imply that associates are to be denied the right to express their concerns. In fact, not allowing associates to express their concerns may increase feelings of frustration and anger. However, seek to address one concern at a time. Associates are politely asked to "wait their turn" until the first concern is addressed. Choose the primary concern and stick to it until it is considered and, hopefully, resolved. This prevents skipping back and forth among issues, which could easily lead to evading the original concern altogether.

Those of us who think invitationally understand that there are no totally objective realities. Everything is viewed from a particular perspective. The other person's reality is just as real as our own. Facts are facts only within some theoretical framework. As explained by Guba (1991), no fact can ever be fully tested because of the challenge of induction. Observing one billion white swans does not provide indisputable evidence for the assertion that "All swans are white." For at that very moment a black swan will appear! No unequivocal explanation is ever possible, so Invitational Leaders keep compromise in mind. Even when every expert in the world agrees, they may all be mistaken. Seeking compromise includes allowing the other person to give full expression to his or her feelings as well, so long as counter-concerns are not introduced during the discussion of the original concern. In other words, stick to one issue at a time.

To confer means to initiate a non-threatening, informal conversation with an associate, in private if at all possible. Conferring begins by signaling, both verbally and non-verbally, that we desire a positive dialogue. These signals are intended to communicate that "I am not here to fight." The idea here is to follow the strategy offered in *Proverbs 1:15*: "A soft answer turneth away wrath; but grievous words stir up anger." The goal is to resolve the concern without having it escalate into a power struggle.

We have invented a simple formula for conferring . We call it "three signals, a wish, and a request." The "three signals" are designed to express a desire for a non-threatening, mutually beneficial dialogue. The three signals serve as simple indicators of peaceful intent. These signals might consist of such things as a soft tone of voice, slow rate of speech, pleasing pitch, a relaxed posture, friendly eye contact, using the person's preferred name, positive choice of words, and perhaps a smile and handshake. The "wish" is to make a clear statement about what is requested. In making a wish, it is vital that it be unambiguous. The value of unambiguous messages was provided by Ulysses S. Grant, the American Civil War General. "No one," stated one Union officer, "ever had to read Grant's orders a second time to understand them." The "request" is to ask that your wish be granted. The surest way to get what we want is to ask for it.

Here is an illustration of how three signals, a wish, and a request might take place. The concern is about an associate who comes to work late. To address the concern, the Invitational Leader stops by the associate's office, smiles, uses the associate's name, comments on some recent success or achievement (the "three signals"), makes a clear and concrete statement (the "wish")—"Harry, I would like for you to get to work on time"—then asks, "Will you do this for me?" (the "request"). When making the request, it is important to be as specific as possible. Obtaining an affirmative response to the request is vital in the event that higher C's might be required.

The reader might question why it is necessary to add "for me" in the request. We think it is necessary because the concern is "our dog." We'll explain with a story. One of the authors and his wife have a lovely walking path near our home. The path meanders through a beautiful glen and we love to take long walks. When we take our walk we are likely to be joined by a neighbor's dog who enjoys our company (Greensboro, North Carolina, where we live, has a firm leash law: "Thou shall keep thy hound on thy leash!"). When the three of us (my wife, the neighbor's dog, and me) pass another couple on the path, with their dog properly attached to a leash, we would receive intentionally disinviting looks. The glares were so bad that we began to explain to people we would meet on the path, "It's not our dog." The statement was repeated so many times it has become almost a tradition in our family. When something comes up that we cannot control, or in which we lack a vested interest, we simply say: "It's not our dog." When we do have a concern, it *is* our dog. Thus, we ask others, "Would you please do this *for me?*" Again, the surest way to get what you want is to ask for it.

Asking others to do things for us is in itself an invitation. It is a generous way of acknowledging our inter-dependence. It is also a recognition that others can ask things of us as well. To illustrate, one of the authors often asks doctoral students to help with research statistics, to obtain subjects for research, or to assist with teaching responsibilities. The result is that the doctoral students have no hesitation asking me for things as well, including reviews of dissertation proposals, advice on preparing teaching portfolios, and letters of recommendation. After the verb "to love," perhaps the most beautiful is "to invite," for it sets the stage for a positive relationship.

Here are some questions we should ask ourselves at the conferring level:

1. Have I clearly indicated what it is that I want?
2. Have I clearly asked that my request be granted?
3. Is there room for compromise or re-conceptualization of the concern?
4. Have I received a clear answer to my request?
5. If my request is refused, do I have sufficient resources to pursue my concern?
6. Are there ways that I might help to resolve the concern?

In most cases, when conferring is used according to the principles of Invitational Leadership (respect, trust, optimism, and intentionality), the situation is resolved in a satisfactory manner. In the unusual case where conferring has not accomplished its purpose, then moving to the third C, "consult," is appropriate.

CONSULT

When faced with situations where conferring has not worked, either because the associate rejected the request or because the associate agreed to the request and did not follow through, then consultation is necessary. In the first situation, where the associate has declined to do what was requested, we have at least defined the situation for both parties. Perhaps now is the time to redirect rather than charge ahead.

An illustration of redirecting a request is provided by police officers. Well-trained police officers are taught that when faced with resistance, they should vary the appeal. Suppose a person is stopped for speeding and the officer detects the smell of alcohol. To make matters worse, the person refuses the police officer's request to step out of the car. In this situation the well-trained officer varies the approach: "Sir, is there anything I can say or do to gain your cooperation here?" Even though police officers possess overwhelming power in the form of stun guns, mace, pepper spray, billy clubs, handcuffs, high-powered revolvers, and more, they are still taught to play their low cards first. They always have the option of moving to higher levels of enforcement should lower levels fail to produce required results. The aim is to find areas of agreement and cooperation wherever possible.

In the second situation, where the associate has agreed to the request but has not followed through, then consultation is necessary. Consultation involves a serious talk about the previous commitment. Applying the same invitational principles, we remind the associate that he or she had agreed to the previous request. We explain the importance of acting on the agreement, we emphasize that his or her previous agreement is important and respected, and then we ask for the order again: "Will you do this for me?" Consulting is more formal and more direct. Here are some questions to ask ourselves:

1. Am I willing to help my associate address the concern?
2. Is the concern of sufficient importance to move to a higher C if necessary?
3. Have the consequences of not resolving the situation been considered by both parties?
4. Do we need assessment time to allow reflection on various courses of action?

5. Is it crystal clear to both parties what is requested?

When a clear and no-nonsense discussion has not resolved the situation, then, reluctantly, it is time to move to an even higher C level: confront.

CONFRONT

Confrontation is a very serious attempt to resolve, or at least manage, a troublesome situation. Because the concern is so serious, it is vital to insure that lower levels of conferring and consulting have not worked before moving into this high-risk confrontation level. While associates may not have as much power as we do, no one is without power. Invitational Leaders move to the confronting level only when the concern is of sufficient importance and earlier efforts to resolve the concern have not worked.

In confronting, we explain again what the original concern is about and what can be done to resolve it. Keeping in mind the principles of Invitational Leadership, we patiently explain that the situation has been addressed previously, the associate has given his or her word that the situation would be resolved, and that the troublesome situation still exists. At the confrontation level it is appropriate to talk about logical consequences. For example: "Harry, you told me that you would get to work on time. You were late again today. Should you be late again, I will place this information in your personnel file. This would damage your chances of future employment. I don't want to do this. Will you please get to work on time for me?" This is a last-ditch effort to solve the concern without resorting to the fifth C: combat.

In the continuing effort to manage the concern, we ask ourselves:

1. Have I made sincere efforts to resolve the concern at each of the lower levels?
2. Do I have documented evidence that shows I have made efforts at lower levels to resolve the concern?
3. Do I have sufficient authority, power, and will to follow through on the consequences *before they are stated*?
4. Have I explored all options to obtain voluntary compliance?
5. Do I have documented evidence that shows I have made efforts at all lower levels to resolve the concern?

When each of the first four levels of concern, confer, consult, and confront have been unsuccessful in resolving the situation, then it is likely that the consequences of confronting are fair and are in keeping with the principles of Invitational Leadership. Should the concern persist in spite of the efforts of the first four C levels, then the fifth C is applied, appropriately and caringly.

COMBAT

It might seem strange that we write about the importance of Invitational Leadership, with its principles of respect, trust, optimism, and intentionality and then present the option of combat. To explain, we use the word *combat* as a verb, not a noun. We wish to combat a troublesome situation, not to enter into combat with an associate. Use of the word *combat* stresses the gravity of the situation. Because the situation has not been resolved at any of the previous four levels, it is now time to move on to logical consequences

Logical consequences are a fact of life. It would be unreasonable to think that a leader can get along with persuasions and explanations alone. There are times when penalties are necessary, from the smallest reprimand to the largest penalty, including demotion and dismissal. But such actions by the leader should be based on real need and clear logic. Real need is established by the fact that all lower "C's" have been tried and have been unsuccessful in resolving the concern. Clear logic seeks to have the penalty make sense to the one being penalized. Efforts should be made to avoid having the person feel wronged and resentful. The only avenue now open is to combat the situation. But even at this difficult stage the Invitational Leader works to maintain respect for associates.

A primary objective of a penalty is to have the offender reflect on the concern, realize what he or she did that was incorrect, and not to do the same thing again. For example, a state trooper pulls us over for exceeding the posted speed limit. The state trooper introduces himself or herself, asks for identification, explains the offense (70 miles per hour in a 45 mile speed zone), and issues a citation. The cost of the speeding ticket is designed to discourage us from future speeding.

Notice here how a well-trained state trooper handles the situation. He or she demonstrates respect for the driver ("May I see your driver's license and auto registration, please?) and uses "Sir" and "Ma'am." When the person who received the ticket drives away, he or she may be angry, but the anger is directed inward, not toward the state trooper. There is a vast difference between a state trooper and a storm trooper.

For obvious reasons, combat should be avoided whenever and wherever possible. At the combat level stakes are high and people are forced into the roles of winners and losers. At this high level it is impossible to predict with absolute assurance who will win and who will lose.

It seems strange to us that some leaders choose combat even when lower "C's" would work as well or better. This is most likely to occur when the leader dislikes an associate, or when the leader dislikes him- or herself. Unfortunately, when leaders use intentionally disinviting processes, it becomes very difficult later to shift downward to a lower C. As someone noted: "When you're winning all the battles and losing the war, it is a sure sign that you don't know what the war is about."

When all else has failed, and combat is necessary, the whispering self should ask:

1. Have I tried all lower levels of conflict management?
2. Is there any hope of compromise, even at this late date?
3. Have I sought advice from fellow leaders and legal experts before reaching this high C note?

People are likely to become angry when they believe that others are treating them unfairly, or that others are seeking to control them. This is particularly true in combat situations. Thus, it is vital that the Invitational Leader keep a consistent stance in accordance with his or her stated philosophy — that people are able, valuable, responsible, and should be treated accordingly — and that the four guiding principles of respect, trust, optimism, and intentionality are followed. This is paramount, particularly in applying the final C: conciliate.

CONCILIATE

After combating a situation, it is important to seek to restore a non-combative relationship. Finding a solution to a particular concern may be insufficient. Ross (1996), in studying indigenous cultures, reported that the crucial part in conflict management is restoring relationships that have been damaged by the situation. If not addressed, this situation can extend far beyond the original conflict. Conflict management, seen this way, is as much about healing as it is about mere resolution. Because leadership is based on human relationships, healing processes are critical components in becoming an Invitational Leader. Combatants and non-combatants alike work to find thoughtful ways to carry on. In some happy situations it is possible to grow from what has occurred. Here are some questions for the whispering self:

1. Do I show respect for associates by not "rubbing it in"?
2. Do I know of helpful intermediaries that could be asked to ameliorate the situation?
3. Do I allow sufficient time and space to pass before attempting to return to normal interactions?
4. Can I arrange for non-threatening activities to be used to restore a sense of community?
5. If a new potentially troublesome situation arises, am I prepared to return to the first C and start the whole process over?

By intentionally following the rule of the C's and striving to manage situations at the lowest possible level with the least expenditure of time and energy, the Invitational Leader is in the best position to avoid acrimony, hostility, and loss of leadership.

The work of inviting oneself professionally is multi-faceted, and it is also a lifelong process. It demands a commitment from the Invitational Leader to continuous learning in a wide variety of fields and subjects, as well as constant exploration for new ideas and fresh knowledge at the boundaries of his or her profession. It demands that the Invitational Leader remain open to change and encourage the same in his or her associates. It demands a willingness to apply innovative practices without fear of failure, to cultivate and nurture meaningful relationships within and outside the workplace, and to strive for a harmonious balance between the personal and the professional. It demands that the Invitational Leader learn to issue invitations in the rain, drawing upon his or her deepest resources to exercise restraint and offer compassion even in the most difficult circumstances. In short, to invite oneself professionally is a crucial step in enjoying fully the rich challenges and rewards of Invitational Leadership.

Chapter Five: Inviting Others Professionally — The Five Powerful P's

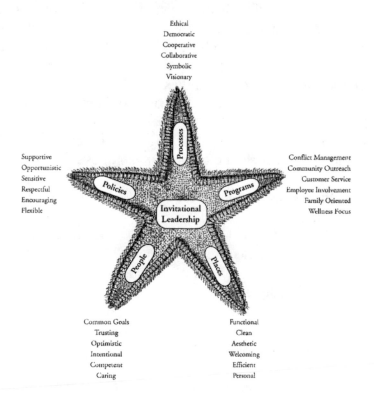

Ethical
Democratic
Cooperative
Collaborative
Symbolic
Visionary

Supportive
Opportunistic
Sensitive
Respectful
Encouraging
Flexible

Conflict Management
Community Outreach
Customer Service
Employee Involvement
Family Oriented
Wellness Focus

Processes

Policies

Programs

Invitational Leadership

People

Places

Common Goals
Trusting
Optimistic
Intentional
Competent
Caring

Functional
Clean
Aesthetic
Welcoming
Efficient
Personal

The starfish lives to eat oysters. To defend itself, the oyster has two stout shells that fit tightly together and are held in place by a powerful muscle. When a starfish locates an oyster it places itself on the top shell. Then gradually, gently, and continuously, the starfish uses each of its five radially disposed arms in turn to keep steady pressure on the one oyster muscle. While one arm works, the others rest. The single oyster muscle, while incredibly powerful, gets no rest. Inevitably and irresistibly, the oyster shell opens and the starfish has its meal. Steady and continuous pressure from a number of points can overcome the strong muscle of the oyster. The starfish illustration offers one analogy for how the Invitational Leader can address each and every part of an organization's structure and culture.

Five powerful factors—people, places, policies, programs, and processes (the five P's)—are highly significant for their separate and combined influence on Invitational Leadership. The combination of these five P's offers an almost limitless number of opportunities for the Invitational Leader, for they address the total culture or ecosystem of almost any organization.

In considering the total influence of the five P's, the Invitational Leader should consider such questions as these:

1. What is the invitational "look" and "feel" of our organization?
2. How do the sounds, smells, and appearance contribute to a welcoming environment?
3. What symbols of respect, trust, and optimism are intentionally evidenced by our policies, programs, and processes?
4. Does our group understand and speak the language of Invitational Leadership?

In creating and maintaining an invitational ecosystem, everything counts.

Frank Lloyd Wright (1954) explained how an ecosystem functions: "Every house worth considering as a work of art must have a grammar of its own. 'Grammar,' in this sense, means the same thing in any construction — whether it be of words or of stone or wood. It is the shape relationship among the various elements that enter into the construction of the thing" (p. 181). Human promises and problems reside within the ecosystem of the five powerful P's.

To think invitationally is to give major attention to the people in the process. At the same time, the Invitational Leader also looks *beyond* people to take into account places, policies, programs, and processes. The secret of Invitational Leadership lies in combining all of these factors into a particular way of functioning, much like stones are joined to make an arch.

Listen to how Marco Polo describes a bridge, stone by stone, to Kublai Khan. "But which is the stone that supports the bridge?" Kublai Khan asks. "The bridge is not supported by one stone or another," Marco answers, "but by the line of the arch that they form." Kublai Khan remains silent, reflecting. Then he adds, "Why do you speak to me of the stones? It is only the arch that matters to me." Marco Polo answers: "Without stones there is no arch" (Calvino, *Invisible Cities*, 1972, p. 82). As the following figure illustrates, the goal in Invitational Thinking is to combine the pieces of a puzzle into a total gestalt.

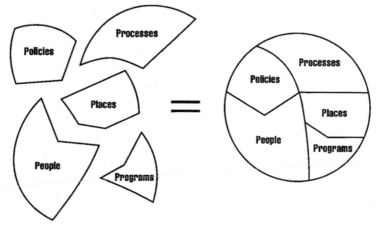

The moment of truth for any organization is when anyone from outside makes any contact with any one of the five
powerful P's, positively or negatively. This contact forms a
long-lasting impression. To think invitationally is to recognize
the significance of the five P's, separately and combined,
beginning with people.

PEOPLE

Being inviting with others professionally requires that
the leader demonstrates intensity of commitment. This in turn
releases the energy of associates. This energy translates the
leader's intentionality into reality and sustains it. As explained
by Nel Noddings (1984), "How good I can be is partly a function of how you—the other— receive and respond to me.
Whatever virtue I exercise is completed, fulfilled in you" (p.
16). What we as leaders hold to be true about our associates
influences what our associates hold to be true about themselves.
The Invitational Leader is one who mobilizes higher levels of
energy in associates, which in turn results in superior performance. Invitational Leadership can only emerge when the gaps
are bridged between leaders and associates.

Inviting others professionally requires cooperation, collaboration, and contribution. The first of these, cooperation,
demonstrates the leader's willingness to work with others for
mutual gain.

COOPERATION

Invitational Leadership is based on working coopera-
tively with others. Cooperation serves as a catalyst to bring us
together in a particular way. In their book on the rites and rituals of corporate life, Deal and Kennedy (1985) reported that
strong organizations are those with a cohesion of values, myths,

heroes, and symbols that tie people together and give meaning and purpose to their day-to-day lives. Cooperation is an invitation to transcend one's isolated existence and reach toward shared goals. It helps us to form a new self-vocabulary, moving from the isolated "I" to the collective "we," "us," and "our."

The opposite of cooperation is competition. In extreme forms, competition can mean to win at any cost, to see the successes of others as one's own failure. As one famous writer is reported to have said: "Every time a friend succeeds I die a little." This harsh view of seeing the world as a rat race, filled with winners and losers, victors and vanquished, is a far cry from Invitational Leadership, where principles of respect, trust, optimism, and intentionality indicate that working for the collective welfare of everyone is the best way to work for one's own welfare.

Of course, organizations themselves must be competitive within their given fields. Colleges compete with one another for students, often playing to particular markets to solidify a customer base, just like a business. They also must compete for resources, both private and public or government money, and so they must learn how best to distinguish themselves in a competitive field. The same holds true for hospitals, and competition in the medical field fuels better practices, better research, and better treatment.

Still, it is important to remember that within the invitational model of leadership this competitive drive to succeed emerges from the basic set of core values that defines an organization. In *Built From Scratch* (1999), Bernie Marcus and Arthur Blank of Home Depot are refreshingly candid about their wish to dominate the market and defeat their closest competitors, but they are equally candid about what drives this fierce desire to win: "We care about each other and we care about the customer. The things that we do for customers inside and outside the stores demonstrate our commitment to them. And then when something happens within the company, we circle the wagons. We help each other." For Marcus and Blank, there is a clear demarcation between winning at all costs and winning within the guidelines of the company's core values. The Invitational Leader never crosses this line, insisting instead on building his or her organization by rallying others to a shared vision of success within a caring environment. He or she makes competition a form of cooperation by offering his or her colleagues a personal and professional stake in the organization's overall success.

The importance of cooperative relations in the work place was demonstrated by the research of Dworkin, Haney, Dworkin, and Telschow (1990). It revealed that physical illness increased as job stress increased, except in organizations where the leadership was viewed as caring, supportive, and cooperative. Relationships between the leader and associates are important factors in both physical and mental health.

Relationships do matter. Leaders who seek cooperation constantly search for common grounds and mutual goals. Results are accomplished without resorting to authoritarian methods. Exercising authority is rarely proportional to the importance of the matter requiring its application. The aim is to have associates willingly, voluntarily, enthusiastically, even *ardently* accept the opportunities we offer.

A tale from ancient India illustrates the value of non-coercive means to accomplish goals. The sun and the wind had an argument about who was more powerful. To test their relative strengths, it was decided that they would hold a contest to see who could make a man remove his coat. The wind blew hard, but the man held tightly onto his coat. The wind then blew at hurricane force, but still the man held desperately to his coat. When it was the sun's turn, the sun smiled warmly on the man, and the man soon removed his coat.

By cordially summoning colleagues to embrace a shared vision of success, Invitational Leaders free the imaginative capabilities of those colleagues. Think about the resources an employee will bring to a job entered into willingly and enthusiastically, as opposed to those brought by an employee who accepts assignments grudgingly. With the highly-functioning brainpower and creativity of an entire team behind his or her projects, the Invitational Leader will find that innovative and resourceful solutions to problems emerge with much greater consistency.

John Clendenin (1989), former chairman and CEO of BellSouth, tells the story of monks building an enormous temple in Kyoto, Japan. Unable to hoist the roof's wooden beams into place, the monks and their followers hit upon an inspiring solution. As Clendenin tells it, "So their thousands of followers grew their hair long, cut it, and wove it into a massive braid—ropes of human hair twelve inches thick. With these braids, the carpenters raised high the roof." Clearly here is a team of workers striving with similar purpose toward a common goal each member has embraced as his or her own.

DELEGATION

The higher leaders go up the ladder of professional success, the more important it is to delegate responsibilities. As most leaders know, workloads, pressures, and responsibilities increase with promotions and seniority. At the same time, the number of hours in a day remain the same. To survive and prevail under such circumstances, it is vital that the Invitational Leader learn how to delegate responsibilities. Delegation is most effective when the principles of respect, trust, optimism, and intentionality are in place.

How delegation of responsibilities demonstrates the principles of Invitational Leadership is explained by Robert Townsend: "Many give lip service, but few delegate authority in important matters. And that means that all they delegate is dog-work. A real leader does as much dog-work for his people as he can. He can do it, or see a way to do without it, ten times as fast. And he delegates as many important matters as he can because they create a climate in which people grow."

According to the *United States Navy Advanced Officer Leadership Manual* (1997), there are five categories of tasks that should be delegated: (1) matters requiring minimal coordination, (2) tasks involving technical knowledge, (3) routine, ongoing matters, (4) matters covered by detailed procedures and policies, and (5) projects with clearly defined results.

When delegating, it is important to give associates breathing room. Allowing associates the freedom of action carries the message that they are able, valuable, and responsible. By stating the desired results, providing "inside" information, and explaining why something is being done, the leader allows associates the freedom to select the manner in which the results will be achieved. If more specific directions must be given, then the Invitational Leader should offer "guiding suggestions" rather than edicts. For example, he or she might begin with a question: "Did you try...," "Would it work to...," "What if you...." Characteristic of Invitational Leadership, these guiding suggestions seek to connect a course of action with an associate's own purposes and intentions. Providing a gentle nudge can usually accomplish more than a hard push.

Here is how General Norman Schwartzkopf explained the value of trust: "I built trust among my components because I trusted them." One of the signs of a truly inviting leader is that he or she is comfortable in delegating responsibilities to associates. In the same vein, Terry Pierce (1995) explained in *Leading out Loud* that successful leaders invite commitment in others: "People must take individual and collective responsibility for both the successes and failures of their organization." Otherwise, the organization will perish.

Cooperation is gained by asking others to do things for us. When leaders try to do everything all by themselves, they are insuring that they will have to do it next time as well, since no one else has had the opportunity to learn how to do it. Frank W. Woolworth, founder of the famous store chain that bears his name, summed up the value of delegation with these words: "I never got far until I stopped imagining I had to do everything myself." Asking for assistance is itself a form of an invitation. It invites others to feel helpful. It also opens the door for others to ask things of us in turn, which is the basis for collaboration.

One word of caution should be mentioned here, and that is the potential danger of "reverse delegation." When the leader accepts responsibility for every decision, associates will be more than happy to let the leader work as hard as she or he desires. Associates will shift decisions to the leader and check with him or her before taking any action. The result is that the leader gets swamped with decision-making of even the most trivial nature, while associates are given a legitimate excuse for inaction. Doing for associates what they can well do for themselves is often disinviting, whether intentional or not. It is also a signal of the leader's distrust in the abilities of associates to handle situations and make decisions.

Successful cooperation establishes trust between leaders and their associates, promoting personal and professional growth at every level of an organization. Indeed, an organization is only as good as the entire team of co-workers who comprise it. For this reason, it is essential for the Invitational Leader to encourage partnerships and teamwork, distributing responsibility for the organization's success as broadly as possible. In his essay "The Secrets of Great Groups," Walter Bennis (1999) stresses the importance of leaders and associates "working toward a shared purpose," citing Luciano de Crescanzo's remark that "we are all angels with only one wing; we can only fly while embracing each other." Bennis concludes, "In the end . . . groups cannot be managed; they can only be led in flight" (p. 322). This is no small responsibility for the Invitational Leader—to lead his or her associates in flight — but if it is undertaken in trust and mutual respect, then surely the flight will be a smooth and graceful one.

Collaboration

Collaboration takes many forms and may be as simple as two people preparing a room for a meeting, car-pooling to a convention, or deciding how to present a program. It might also be collaboration among national organizations, such as the American Psychological Association and the American Counseling Association, who work together in preparing testing standards. The underlying principle is that parties work together for the benefit of both. A colleague referred to the importance of collaboration as the "Canoe theory." People are less likely to bore holes when they're in the boat with you. An important part of collaboration is to keep associates informed.

Keeping associates informed demonstrates both respect and trust. Conversely, withholding information is a sign of disrespect and distrust. In fact, withholding information is often used as a way of punishing other people or sabotaging their efforts. As Schaub (1991) pointed out, for some, poor communication is more deliberate than accidental. Withholding information and knowledge from others is an effective way to deny them power. In the absence of information, misunderstandings and rumors flourish. The best way to provide information and stamp out rumors immediately is to give full and complete facts wherever and whenever possible.

Staying in contact and keeping associates informed requires the Invitational Leader not get too far ahead or out of reach of associates. The trick is to raise levels of aspirations and expectations while maintaining contact with followers. To appreciate present successes while pointing the way toward future goals, though, is a little like sailing between the *Scylla* and the *Charybdis*, but it can be done. Appreciating present accomplishments involves recognizing associates for their past and present successes. Saluting the contributions of others encourages future accomplishments.

COMMITMENT

An Invitational Leader is a bold and passionate activist. This requires a commitment to action. It is his or her responsibility to make things happen, rather than await the happening. The goal of Invitational Leadership is to create dynamic situations which summon others to respond in certain ways. No great leader accepts things as they are. If they do, they are no longer leaders, but are instead simply administrators and functionaries to a system. The role of an Invitational Leader is to demonstrate commitment through his or her vision of greatness.

A good example of Invitational Leadership in action can be found at the *New Yorker*, where there is a long-standing tradition of calling cartoonists "artists." The happy result is that many *New Yorker* cartoonists have become well-known artists. The power of the leader is to make invitations so vivid and appealing that they are voluntarily and enthusiastically accepted.

A classic lack of vision was provided by the early movie producer Harry Warner. When he heard about plans to break the sound barrier in films (to create "talkies"), he argued: "Who the hell wants to hear actors talk?" To accomplish great things, an Invitational Leader is required to see clearly what is, but also to see what is coming — to be a futurist in his or her thinking.

Leaders have the opportunity to have great dreams, and they have the commitment to make these dreams come true. John Dewey called this leadership quality "a new audacity of imagination." Invitational Leaders enroll associates in a vision of greatness, offering them a vivid and compelling picture of their relatively boundless potential. They summon associates to higher levels of functioning and the construction of something of mutual benefit. This acknowledges both our commitment and our interdependence.

No greater example of commitment and interdependence can be found than in Shakespeare's Henry V's stirring address to a small group of adherents on the eve of the forthcoming Saint Crispin's day battle:

> We few, we happy few, we band of brothers...
> And gentlemen in England now a-bed
> Shall think themselves accurs'd they were not here
> And hold their manhoods cheap whiles any speak
> That fought with us upon Saint Crispin's day. (Act IV, scene III)

Human beings require something fulfilling to live for. Perhaps the greatest invitation in human existence is to find meaning, direction, and purpose in life. Thus, the Invitational Leader is one who summons associates to seek and achieve a life of rich significance.

CONTRIBUTIONS

Those who think invitationally derive satisfaction from the contributions they make to the welfare of those they seek to serve. They measure their success by the extent to which their efforts make places, policies, programs, and processes more receptive, accommodating, and sensitive to people.

Being professionally inviting with others by cooperating, collaborating, and contributing embraces ideals found in many spiritual, humanistic, existential, and democratic orientations. Judeo-Christian beliefs regarding love for one another, the humanistic concepts of social interest and individual potential, the existential thoughts regarding existence and the self, and the democratic values of liberty and justice — all are compatible with Invitational Leadership. Leaders who invite others professionally are in the best position to extend themselves in cooperative, collaborative, and contributing ways.

Becoming and being an Invitational Leader is a journey,

not a destination. We constantly reinvent ourselves, as the main character in Gabriel Garcia Marquez's (1988) *Love in The Time of Cholera* discovers: "[H]e allowed himself to be swayed by his conviction that human beings are not born once and for all on the day their mothers give birth to themselves, but that life obliges them over and over again to give birth to themselves." The goal is to realize our potential in all areas of worthwhile human endeavor.

Invitational Leaders are successful through their primary emphasis on people. Some leaders who follow other approaches to leading have been known to make decisions based on efficiency, effectiveness, and conformity, rather than basing decisions on respect for people. Examples include a "No food or drink" rule for waiting rooms (to keep the rooms neat and clean), "Reserved parking" for administrators (while visitors are made to park in distant lots), and "No checks accepted" (to simplify bookkeeping). These decisions are often made for the convenience of those in authority at the inconvenience of many. An extreme example of this sort of "convenience" thinking occurred when the Japanese attacked Pearl Harbor on December 7, 1941. American military personnel had a hard time defending themselves against their attackers because their ammunition had been locked up for the sake of convenient accountability and security.

Invitational Leaders maintain a proper regard for places, policies, programs, and processes, but people come first. It is vital to alter, whenever and wherever possible, factors that demonstrate lack of trust and respect for people, or that inhibit their optimal functioning.

A concern for people becomes even more critical in an age where technology is increasingly dominant. The computer revolution and other marvelous events of our time must be balanced with a proper regard for the people in the process. Here is how Waitley (1995) in his book *Empires of the Mind* expressed a warning: "[T]he new technologies ... especially since they're coming at a time when the world is much advanced in human rights and well versed in consumerism ... can have little economic or social value unless they're combined with, or grounded in, understanding of human ways and needs" (p. 18). New technologies will not succeed in business or society unless greater, not less, attention is given to people.

Think, for instance, of the impact of technology on the world of higher education. While it no doubt makes the work of research much easier and more efficient, making possible new and advanced developments in mathematics and the sciences, it should not be considered a substitute for more traditional styles of teaching and learning. A university is more than an information center. Although it is commonly argued that advances in technology make communication easier, these changes cannot substitute for direct and lively conversation. In fact, technology eliminates the need for face-to-face encounters and often distances us from our colleagues. Collegiality is the hallmark of the university life, a time-honored tradition that is continually recreated by new friendships and new learning. In the multicultural world of today's academic environment, it is more urgent than ever that colleagues engage one another and their students in meaningful and productive dialogue. In an invitational model of higher education, technology becomes a supplement to the true work of collegiality.

We should remember, too, that no matter how advanced technology might become, there will always be a need for what might be called the "human touch," especially in organizations that provide crucial services to the general public. One of the authors experienced the difference an inviting, human presence can make while working as a consultant for a large hospital. An elderly male patient had been moved into the hospital corridor on a wheeled stretcher and left there, perhaps to be moved later to another place for medical treatment. As he lay there, a burly hospital electrician, complete with leather belt and dangling tools, came striding down the corridor. When the electrician spotted the elderly patient, he stopped and struck up a friendly conversation. The electrician asked the patient if there was anything he could do for him. The patient replied that he felt cold and would like a blanket. The electrician walked over to the nurses' station, obtained a blanket, and very caringly placed it over the patient. At that moment the electrician was as much a health provider as any physician in the hospital. Indeed, people are paramount in Invitational Leadership, taking priority over places, policies, programs, and processes. They are valuable in and of themselves, with no need for "because."

PLACES

Deal and Kennedy (1985), in their book *Corporate Cultures: The Rites and Rituals of Corporate Life*, pointed out that successful organizations bind people together and give meaning and purpose to their lives. This cohesion is facilitated by inviting places. People shape buildings, and in turn buildings shape the people who live and work there.

The physical environment is a socially constructed support system in which people develop ideas about themselves. They receive countless signals from this communication medium that tell them how much the people who design, build, operate, maintain, and manage the physical environment respect them, trust them, and care about them. Human beings are far more sensitive to their physical environments than they may seem. Gladwell (2000) calls this sensitivity to places the "power of context." The physical setting represents a highly significant but often overlooked leadership resource.

Developing a welcoming physical environment involves creating and maintaining a clean, comfortable, and safe setting. It also means that the leader works to insure that rooms, hallways, and commons areas are adequately lighted and heated, have plenty of fresh air, and have comfortable furniture. Even the space between buildings defines the place as much as the architecture. In his book *The Spaces Between Buildings*, Larry Ford (2000) stated that in considering places it is important to consider alleys, porches, gardens, loading docks, rooftops, walkways, and nooks and crannies. Leaders who think invitationally find ways to improve the physical environment, even when voices say that "nothing can be done." Challenging these defeatist voices is where Invitational Leadership begins.

To think invitationally is to make things happen. Invitational Leaders keep a close eye on how to make things happen through the physical environment, for places that add to, or subtract from, respect for people. The importance of the physical environment was recognized by Thomas Jefferson, who worried more about the physical setting of his University of Virginia than he did about the curriculum. He worked to design buildings that encouraged the classical ideals of conversation and interaction between students and faculty. By placing the housing of faculty directly in contact with student housing, Jefferson wanted faculty to observe students, and for students to have ample opportunity to observe their professors at work and at play.

In her case analysis of collegiate leadership and cultural change, Anna Neumann (1995) suggested that although leaders may not be able to affect change in others directly, they may do so by changing the place. By altering the physical setting, leaders create a situation that invites participants to think differently about what they are doing and why they are doing it. Equally important, by altering the physical environment in a substantial way, new behaviors and non-routine thinking are encouraged. Individuals are connected to their physical environments. The places in which people find themselves have an impact on morale, satisfaction, productivity, creativity, and customer service.

An assessment of the physical environment will identify variables that can be modified, adjusted, and improved. A fresh coat of paint, positively-worded signs, arrows pointing to offices and bathrooms, new curtains, improved lighting, clean carpets, appropriate decorations, conveniently-located trash cans, rearrangement of furniture, good ventilation, and clean windows can produce highly beneficial results. One reception- ist reported that when the tall counter and plate glass that divid- ed her office were removed and replaced with an attractive receptionist's station, she felt as if she had been let out of prison.

Places take on a life of their own. Some places are fully alive and vibrant, some are not. Some have personalities, with welcoming energy. Others are lackluster and dreary. Physical squalor contributes to "burnout," the process whereby people lose their sense of value, ability, and responsibility. As Pines and Aronson (1981) note: "Burnout is not a function of bad peo- ple who are cold and uncaring. It is a function of bad situations in which once idealistic people must operate. It is then that sit- uations must be modified so that they promote, rather than destroy, human values" (p. 61). There are no excuses for dirty rest rooms, crowded cafeterias, full trash cans, smoke-filled rooms, dark hallways and parking lots, mortuary lighting, unkempt offices, broken furniture, peeling paint and plaster, and self-induced squalor.

A particularly disinviting part of places is the signs that attempt to direct behavior. Consider the emotional impact of these signs:

KEEP OUT!
WE DO NOT GIVE CHANGE.
OUT OF ORDER.
KEEP THIS DOOR SHUT!
NO MORE THAN TWO GARMENTS IN
DRESSING ROOM.
TAKE A NUMBER AND BE SEATED.
NO TICKET, NO LAUNDRY.
CASH ONLY.

The above are all examples of disinviting signs.

Invitational Leaders recognize that excuses do not free

us from responsibilities. The easiest thing in the world is to create an excuse. To illustrate: Once there was a farmer whose cow went dry, producing no milk. The farmer walked down the lane to a nearby farm and asked the neighbor if he could borrow some milk. The neighbor replied that he would like to loan some milk, but he did not have any rope with which to tie it. The startled farmer exclaimed: "You don't need rope to tie up milk!" And the neighbor replied: "When you don't want to do something, one excuse is as good as another." As Invitational Leaders, we accept responsibility for our habitats.

In considering places, what really seems to matter the most are the little things. As stated by Gladwell (2000), "If a window is broken and left un-repaired, people walking by will conclude that no one cares and no one is in charge. Soon, more windows will be broken, and the sense of anarchy will spread from the building to the street on which it faces, sending a signal that anything goes. A broken window is an invitation to serious crime. The secret is to quickly remove graffiti, replace broken windows, and arrest small-time violators, such as those who jump turnstiles to beat subway fares" (p. 141). Sometimes, the tiniest difference in process can become a major difference in outcome. To illustrate: The New York City Police Department discovered that by removing graffiti as quickly as it appeared, the crime rate in the area was lowered. How people behave is in large measure a function of the places they inhabit.

Improving the physical environment may not quickly lead to benefits, but it is important that the total place be continuously assessed, alternatives explored, and necessary improvements made. Maintaining a special awareness of the place was described by the song and dance man, George Burns (1976), and is worth repeating here.

One night at a party George Burns saw a fellow dancer standing in a hallway. Burns asked, "Charles, why are you standing out there? Come on in." Charles said, 'No, George, this parquet floor has a nice feel to it." Burns goes on to explain: "Now, nobody else would have understood that, but right away, I knew exactly what he meant. It was a dancer's floor. So I went out there and stood with him, and Charles was right. It was the nicest floor I ever stood on" (p. 85-86). Leaders who think invitationally are alert to the total physical environment, particularly the little things.

Fortunately, the easiest thing an Invitational Leader can do is to change the physical environment. Almost everyone can agree that a hallway is dingy, a bathroom is unpleasant, an office is unattractive, the cafeteria is grimy, an entrance way is cluttered, the grounds are unkempt. Because physical environments are so obvious in their appearance, they are usually the quickest thing to change. Changing the setting offers a golden opportunity to make immediate improvements and thus invite others professionally.

Questions that the Invitational Leader might ask himself or herself about the physical environment include:

1. Do people feel a part of this place?
2. Do they take ownership of it?
3. Would I want to bring my family here?
4. Does this physical environment make sense?
5. Why would anyone like to come here?
6. What might people learn by coming to this place?

Obviously, the physical place should contribute to a sense of belonging and ownership. As DePree (1989) noted in *Leadership is an Art*, the places we create are usually a consequence of the thinking we employ to build and maintain them.

POLICIES

Policies are everywhere, issued by government agencies, executive boards, councils, C.E.O.'s, administrators, supervisors, presidents, deans, provosts, legislators, commanding officers, sergeants, captains, generals, admirals, and count-less others. Unavoidably, the policies we create, whether enforced or unenforced, formal or informal, reasonable or unreasonable, communicate powerful messages of trust or dis-trust, respect or disrespect, optimism or pessimism. Policies, like places, reveal the thinking of those who create and enforce them.

People and places are influenced by the regulations, guidelines, commands, codes, orders, mandates, limits, plans, rules, and edicts that regulate the ongoing functions of organi-zations and fill our modern world. Sometimes, policies are cre-ated that, although well-meaning, place undue restrictions and burdens on people. Scott Adams' cartoon character *Dilbert* highlights the necessary stupidity of out-of-touch, centralized, and remote administrators. Leaders who think invitationally understand how policies affect people, and they use this under-standing to develop policies that facilitate human functioning. The following example illustrates how a thoughtless policy, although small in itself, can have costly consequences.

Several years ago a committee was appointed by the International Alliance for Invitational Education, a not-for-prof-it educational association, to select the site for a future world conference on Invitational Education. The committee visited the Koury Convention Center in Greensboro, North Carolina, which was its first choice. After taking a guided tour of Koury's beautiful facilities, the committee met at a cafeteria in the Koury Center to have a cup of coffee and consider the Center's suitability for the Alliance Conference. The commit-tee members paid for their coffee and proceeded down the serv-ing line to fill their cups. On the coffee urn was a big black and white poster: "NO REFILLS!" The committee talked about this very disinviting sign and wondered, "What would happen if someone really wanted a refill?" After discussing the sign, and considering the mentality of the manager who would allow such a sign to be posted, the committee decided that the Koury Convention Center was no place for an Invitational Education

Conference. The Greensboro Marriott Hotel was chosen instead, and the Koury Convention Center lost the business associated with hosting a large conference.

Even the smallest policy can serve as a "tipping point." When policies place unreasonable, insensitive, or uncaring restrictions on people, they detract from the overall potential of the organization. Moreover, they sometimes contribute to the difficulties encountered by the very people they are designed to serve.

PROGRAMS

Developing and managing programs is a necessary part of any leader's responsibility. Salary incentive programs, wellness programs, training seminars, retirement programs, recruitment programs, and countless other programs contribute to the goals and objectives of any organization.

Regrettably, it sometimes happens that well-meaning and high-minded programs harm individuals or groups because they focus too narrowly on one dimension, while overlooking or neglecting the wide perspective of human needs. To illustrate, some programs have been built around "minimum standards," where production quotas are rigidly enforced. The result is that minimum standards become maximum goals. Industrial workers have been known to heavily penalize those who exceed the minimum workload assigned to the group.

An example of the dangers involved in minimum standards was provided by Hal G. Lewis, a friend of the authors. Hal said that when he was a college student he was hired to work on a dock unloading arriving trucks. One day he noticed that a fork-lift was on the dock and figured that by using the lift he and his co-workers could unload ten times as many boxes in the same time period. He and co-workers could unload a large number of boxes in one fell swoop, saving a great deal of time and energy. When he suggested this idea to his fellow workers, they replied that they were not paid to think, and that he should keep his ideas to himself. There is a danger in programs that treat people as mindless functionaries to a system and discourage them from being effective. When people are treated as objects, they are likely to sabotage the system. Consider this additional example.

A major American university issued "warranties" on teachers that graduated from their School of Education. If, for any reason, a new teacher was not performing adequately at his or her new teaching position, the university would dispatch professors to "fix" the young teacher. Many of these young teachers resented being treated as objects to be fixed. From an invitational perspective, warranties and guarantees are for batteries, light bulbs, bathtubs, and lawn mowers, but not for people.

The value of respectful and trustful programs was documented by Ouchi (1981), who developed a program for successful management which he named "Theory Z." This popular theory of management affirms the value of collaborative decision making, mutual trust, and a warm and caring collegiality. Moreover, Theory Z programs emphasize minimal managerial supervision. Employees who are treated as able, valuable, and responsible are likely to behave accordingly.

PROCESSES

The final powerful P in Invitational Leadership, process, is embedded in the places, policies, programs, and people considered earlier. But process is so important that it deserves recognition in its own right. Process is more than the lyrics of an organization — it represents the melody. By analogy, it is the air in which the birds fly, the water in which fish swim, the forests in which the animals live — it is the *context* in which things happen. For example, when we drink a glass of water, the water is the content, but the glass is the context. It provides the structure or containment for the water. Process represents not only the content of what is offered, but also the context.

Invitational Leadership is itself a process. It reveals itself in the countless ways the other four P's function. To give an example, one of the authors was meeting with a dean regarding a difficult situation. The dean proclaimed, "Well, I got the job done." To which the author replied, "Yes, but you did not get the job done in the right way." How something is accomplished is as important as what is accomplished.

In thinking invitationally, each and every process is evaluated by asking these questions:

1. Does the process demonstrate respect for individual uniqueness and cultural diversity?
2. Does the process reflect a cooperative spirit where people care about each other and assist those who may need special assistance?
3. Does it encourage a sense of belonging where everyone thinks in terms of *our* organization, *our* traditions, *our* colleagues, and *our* responsibilities?
4. Does the process reflect positive expectations that encourage feelings of self-control and individual decision-making?
5. Does the process encourage democratic interactions among members of the organization and the larger community?

These questions assist the Invitational Leader in measuring the effectiveness of his or her organization against its core values. Of course, they should ideally be asked by every associate and employee at every stage of a given process, so that in the end there is consistency at every level of the organization. If the core values of Invitational Leadership have been successfully absorbed into the organization's processes, then every project will be carried forward according to shared goals and objectives, in a spirit of cooperation and collegiality.

In considering processes, it is useful to compare and

contrast two organizational metaphors, the "inviting family" and the "efficient factory." The former is defined by processes fully integrated with invitational core values, while the latter highlights the costs of functioning without an overarching moral or ethical philosophy—specifically, a philosophy that considers people as an organization's most valuable resource. The processes revealed in each of these metaphors can help us to understand this concept's central place in the theory of Invitational Leadership.

THE INVITING FAMILY

As mentioned in chapter one, the word "invitation" comes from the Latin *invitare*, which means "to summon cordially, not to shun." This meaning is essential to positive family relationships, in which each family member is summoned to realize his or her unique potential and no one in the family is shunned. Indeed, the metaphor of the inviting family can stand in for any organization whose processes allow for positive personal and professional growth. The inviting family does not have a standardized form; however, it does have at least six characteristics: (1) respect for individual uniqueness, (2) cooperative spirit, (3) sense of belonging, (4) pleasing habitat, (5) positive expectations, and (6) vital connections to society. Let us consider these characteristics in turn, keeping in mind how they would also form a compelling model for any business or organization.

RESPECT FOR INDIVIDUAL UNIQUENESS.

The inviting family appreciates individual differences. Not everyone is expected to be alike or to do the same thing. Family members who are unable or unwilling to meet traditional expectations or aspirations are tolerated. "He's not heavy, he's my brother" is a phrase that reflects this attitude of support. There is also shared pride in those who exceed the family's fondest hopes. In the inviting family, the invitational principles of respect, trust, optimism, and intentionality are pervasive.

COOPERATIVE SPIRIT.

"One for all and all for one" describes the inviting family. Adults and children learn from each other. The family is seen by all its members as a cooperative enterprise in which cooperation is valued over competition. When one member succeeds, all members feel a part of the success. And when one member is having difficulty, it is a family concern. Everyone pitches in to help until the person is able to participate more fully. In the inviting family, a special watch is kept for those in the family who might need a special boost. This support is provided within a circle of unconditional respect for the feelings of those who may need assistance.

SENSE OF BELONGING.

A most important quality of the inviting family is a deep sense of belonging. This feeling is cultivated wherever possible. Family members spend time talking with each other and sharing their feelings and concerns. They make a special effort to look beyond their own immediate gratification to the needs of other family members. Everyone thinks in terms of *our* family, *our* home, *our* traditions, *our* responsibilities. This loyalty and warmth result in mutual appreciation, positive self-esteem, and a deep sense of family togetherness.

PLEASING HABITAT.

Aesthetics are given a high priority in the inviting family. Living green plants, attractive colors, comfortable furniture, soft lighting, open space, cleanliness, pleasant smells, fresh air, and comfortable temperatures are provided wherever possible. Changes in the physical environment are made regularly to keep the habitat interesting and attractive. The emphasis on creating a pleasing aesthetic environment, even in the most difficult situations, is beautifully illustrated by Betsy Smith (1943) in her book *A Tree Grows in Brooklyn*, in which a poor family obtains a piano at great effort and sacrifice. In the inviting family's habitat, everything is designed to send the message: "Be as comfortable as possible. We're glad you're here."

POSITIVE EXPECTATIONS.

Encouraging each family member to realize his or her unique potential is an important quality of the inviting family. Family members expect good things of themselves and others, but these expectations are always presented within an atmosphere of respect. Every effort is made to encourage feelings of self-control and individual responsibility.

VITAL CONNECTIONS TO SOCIETY.

The inviting family is not insulated from the larger society. Individual family members have wide and various interactions in the world and bring back ideas to share with the rest of the family. There is much excitement and growth is essential. Each member is encouraged to realize his or her unique potential and no one in the family is shunned. Now let's compare the inviting family with the traditional efficient factory model.

THE EFFICIENT FACTORY

Although one model obviously cannot stand in for all industries, there has been a traditional emphasis on the following six characteristics in interpretations of the philosophy underpinning factory work: (1) mass production, (2) uniform product, (3) cost effectiveness, (4) technology, (5) centralized control, and (6) workers as functionaries. It will be interesting to consider these processes in turn, especially their effect on factory workers.

MASS PRODUCTION.

In the efficient factory, a large number of units, all alike, are turned out by assembly lines. In some cases, depending on a marketing analysis and the promotional activities of the sales department, minor differences in appearance and performance are introduced. But these differences are in various models and not in individual units coming off the line. The major emphasis is on quantity. Raw materials are graded, hammered, shaped, processed, conditioned, and turned into a standard and uniform product.

UNIFORM PRODUCT.

The efficient factory is supervised closely to ensure that each product meets minimum standards of quality and sameness. The process requires many experts who are charged with insuring quality control. These experts monitor, sample, test, and approve or reject goods. Products that are damaged in the factory process, or that differ in any significant way, are rejected and shoved side. These rejects will later be recycled, destroyed, or marked down and sold at discount as irregulars, odd lots, close-outs, or seconds, often without brand name or identification. These inferior goods, sometimes found in factory outlets, damaged goods stores, discount houses, or flea markets, fail to meet the minimum required standards of uniformity and quality.

COST EFFECTIVENESS.

In the efficient factory, the highest priority is cost effectiveness. The aesthetics of the plant are relatively unimportant. Factories are designed without windows to control the climate, reduce maintenance, and prevent vandalism and theft. Efficient factories are often surrounded by chain-link fences topped with barbed wire and have gates with guards on duty around the clock. Cost corners are cut wherever possible, and short-term profits are sometimes given priority over long-range planning. In almost every policy decision, cost is the bottom line.

TECHNOLOGY.

Technological advances are greatly valued in the efficient factory and are introduced into plants as quickly as possible. Considerable attention is paid to such hardware items as computers, automatic equipment, programmed delivery systems, and other inventions designed to provide swift and sure processing. Even workers are seen as physical objects to be combined with the latest machinery to provide still more technological efficiency.

CENTRALIZED CONTROL.

In the efficient factory, planning is usually separated from production. Authority flows from the top down, from boards to executives, to production managers, to plant superintendents, to supervisors, and finally to workers. Policies and programs are traditionally developed in places and by people far removed from the production line in function and status, if not in distance. Managers and workers have their respective functions and prerogatives, and workers have little voice in planning. Workers make gains when they can by organizing, bargaining, and, when necessary, by striking. But whatever workers gain, it usually does not include a role in policy formulation and program design. This formulation is done by boards of directors, executive management, and design experts.

WORKERS AS FUNCTIONARIES.

Workers in the efficient factory are expected to be punctual, obedient, conforming, and, above all, *busy*. Individual needs, interests, and personalities are relatively unimportant. Work is broken into small, easy-to-understand, mistake-proof tasks. The workers schedules are controlled by clocks, bells, buzzers, whistles, shifts, public address systems, assembly lines, and a host of supervisors. Efficiency studies are made regularly to monitor the entire process to ensure maximum pro-duction. Meanwhile, public relations departments project the image of the happy worker.

These efficient factory characteristics are certainly not comprehensive or universal, but they do suggest the processes found in the traditional industrial plant. Such organizations have produced an avalanche of material goods, much of it good and some of it shoddy. In return for this cornucopia of prod-ucts, the world has paid a heavy price in human suffering, dis-content, and environmental pollution and destruction.

Clearly we've stacked the deck in presenting these two contrasting examples—the inviting family and the efficient fac-tory—but we haven't offered any information that does not accurately represent processes that exist in real-life organiza-tions. Indeed, the factory model is one that is based on a care-fully developed philosophy of the successful business, one that revolves around profit as the bottom line. Money becomes the most important resource, and people—the employees who make the profit possible but receive little benefit from it—are merely cogs in a well-oiled machine. The factory model also reminds us of the worst aspects of hierarchical leadership, where the chairman or CEO is so far removed from the daily operations on the factory floor that he or she rarely if ever engages employees on a personal level. The employees in turn will begin to realize just how small a stake they have in the suc-cess of the organization, becoming distrustful and resentful of the leadership.

Earlier in this chapter, we discussed the competitive ethos of the Home Depot, whose processes could not be any different from those of the efficient factory. A business need not diminish the importance of competition and profit in order to build an environment resembling that of the inviting family. Home Depot is the perfect example of such a company. Think, for instance, of the words we quoted earlier from Bernie Marcus and Arthur Blank (1999): "When something happens within the company, we circle the wagons. We help each other." With this invitational attitude toward associates, Marcus and Blank have established a strong cooperative spirit, encouraged a sense of belonging among co-workers, and reinforced the positive expectations they have for their associates. Employees treated in this way will be moved to embrace the company's overall vision, learn to respect the company's leadership, and strive to support their co-workers as everyone works on projects of mutual benefit.

Process is the bottom line in Invitational Leadership, for it reveals how the other four P's fit together to support a culture of respect, trust, optimism, and intentionality. As Gandhi reminded us, "Take care of the means, and the ends will take care of themselves." As the example of the inviting family makes clear, the process in which an invitation is embedded is as important as the invitation itself.

Invitational Leadership is not an accident. It is the intentional product of people, places, policies, programs, and processes working together. Those who think invitationally are most likely to be successful when they consider all the factors that influence human existence and potential. As we have discussed previously, an Invitational Leader will learn a great deal about human potential and motivation by first turning inward and discovering his or her true meaning as a person. In the final analysis, leadership must first be anchored in becoming and being a decent human being. The first invitation the Invitational Leader offers is to the self.

CHAPTER SIX:
INVITING OURSELVES PERSONALLY

Here, you see, is the greatest, the most inglorious default, namely to encounter the nothingness represented by one's lack of essence and to interpret this lack as a kind of deformity to be corrected or made up for by others. It is precisely the opposite of a deformity! The lack is an invitation to be—an invitation to be something worth being, an invitation to fill up the nothingness with an essence that is worthy of existing and undeserving of being lost.

—Van Cleave Morris (1966), *Existentialism in Education,*
What It Means (p. 28)

This chapter considers the person of the Invitational Leader and explains what is necessary to sustain the desire and energy to function consistently at an intentionally inviting level. Leaders are in a much better position to care for others when they first care for themselves. Specifically, leaders who think invitationally work to be personally inviting with themselves emotionally, physically, intellectually, and semantically.

Indeed, to care for oneself is often more difficult than to care for others. In a study by Wiemer and Purkey (1994), it was reported that individuals tend to be far more understanding, forgiving, and supportive of others than they are of themselves.

133

Moreover, these same individuals tend to be much more repressive, punitive, and harsh toward themselves than they are toward others. To overcome this bias, it is helpful to remind ourselves not to feel guilty when we are being personally inviting with ourselves.

The value of being personally inviting with ourselves was beautifully expressed by Coudert:

> The single relationship truly central and crucial in a life is the relationship to the self. It is rewarding to find someone whom you like, but it is essential to like yourself. It is quickening to recognize that someone is a good and decent human being, but it is indispensable to view yourself as acceptable. It is a delight to discover people who are worthy of admiration and respect and love, but it is vital to believe yourself deserving of these things. (p. ll8)

Perhaps a reminder of the value of being inviting with ourselves is provided by airline flight attendants who instruct passengers: "In case of the loss of cabin pressure, a mask will drop down from the ceiling. You first place the mask over your own face, then place a mask over the face of your children." The message is clear: Take care of ourselves first so we can take better care of others.

We as leaders understand the message, but we think we simply don't have time to heed the message. We're too busy generating, too busy with much doing, and we often neglect the very responsibilities we most need to meet—keeping ourselves healthy, relatively stress-free, intellectually curious, personally fulfilled. In chapter four, we discussed at some length the importance to Invitational Leaders of continuous learning and continuous exploration (or insight and outsight). These are equally important in any quest for personal meaning and significance, and they fit perfectly into a general scheme of personal development. Inviting ourselves personally means making sure we take time for ourselves and our family and friends, avoiding the kind of obsessive ambitiousness that is destructive to the personal life.

The dangers of overweening ambition are perhaps nowhere more evident than in today's corporate, high-tech workplace. Many among America's younger working generation are blurring the line between work and the rest of life, setting a trend in motion that seems to be taking over the whole of the country. In her essay "Ecstatic Capitalism's Brave New Work Ethic," Kay S. Hymowitz (2001) makes a compelling case that our society is deliberately structured now to emphasize work at the expense of all other activity:

> Airports are outfitted with computer connections, fax machines, and work stations; planes and trains are simply cubicles that happen to be speeding through cumulus clouds and fields of green while you make business calls and work your spreadsheet. And when you arrive at even the most alluring destination, you simply settle into another office away from the office: Marriott hotels have installed more than 20,000 "Rooms that Work" with special desks, phone jacks, ergonomic chairs, and around-the-room Internet access. (p. 3)

Among the casualties for those who pursue this kind of work-obsessed lifestyle are families and friendships. As Hymowitz notes, the contemporary workplace often attempts to take the place of traditional domestic life. One corporate head even goes so far as to warn his new recruits of this reality: "You could stay home, raise the kids, go to college, write the Great American Novel, or slit your wrists and end it all . . . . My job is to make sure that I'm providing you with a combination of economic, psychic, and emotional benefits that makes working for [us] better than anything else you can do" (p. 8). Notice how this corporate head assumes that working for his company

should take precedence over family, education, art, self-confi-
dence — over life itself!

This is not to say that work does not provide personal
fulfillment—indeed, as we described in chapter five, inviting
ourselves professionally is a key step in the process of living a
rewarding and meaningful life. Yet only the most hard-hearted
among us would disagree that it is from our personal relationships that we derive the most sustaining joy. What professional accomplishment can compare with the thrill of exchanging
vows with a life partner or welcoming a new child into the
world? There must be balance, granted, and professional success undoubtedly can give us a sense of confidence and self-
worth that carries over into our personal relationships. Still, we
would do well to remember the age-old adage about the consequences of "all work and no play."

The Invitational Leader never takes personal life for
granted. Honoring the personal as well as the professional are
invitational *principles* of the truly well-lived life. It is instructive that Stephen Covey (1991) devotes significant space to a
discussion of family life in his *Principle-centered leadership.*
Covey states the matter boldly: "Professional successes can't
compensate for failures in marriage and family relationships;
life's ledger will reflect the imbalance, if not the debt" (p. 130).

To Covey's credit, he does not oversimplify the work
involved in maintaining rich and rewarding family relationships. It is complex work, to be sure, as he reminds us: "It
takes patience, self-control, and courage balanced with consideration. In short, it takes considerable maturity and the exercise
of our higher faculties" (p. 139). It also takes time, a commod-
ity seemingly in short supply these days. With more and more
parents pulling double duty at the workplace, time for family
interaction has decreased markedly. In a recent column, George
Will cites one study which reports that "between 1965 and the
late 1980s, the amount of time the average child spent interacting with a parent declined 43 percent, from 30 hours a week to
around 17."

One can speculate with some confidence that the figures would be similar for the decline in the amount of "quality" time couples spend together. And if we cannot find time for our spouses and families, how on earth will we follow Covey's advice to "cultivate the ability to be alone and to think deeply, ... reflect, write, listen, plan, visualize, ponder, relax" (p. 140)? The very thought must seem ludicrous to the well-seasoned CEO. Yet the culprit in each of these cases—stealing time away from our spouses, family, and ourselves—is increased responsibility (often self-imposed) in the workplace.

Reversing these trends will take a conscious decision on the part of those whose families and friendships are suffering the consequences. If such a decision is not made, as Covey says, "the ledger will reflect the imbalance," and the after-effects might manifest themselves years later in any number of ways—in stress-related illness, say, or depression, or spiritual crisis. If we complain that we cannot find the time to meet our deepest personal needs, then perhaps we should review our schedules, readjust our priorities, and determine to put truly first things first. Perhaps we should learn to invite ourselves *personally*.

In being personally inviting with ourselves it is necessary to keep in mind Invitational Leadership's principles of respect, trust, optimism, and intentionality. Caring for ourselves reflects these principles and provides us with the strength to care for others.

INVITING OURSELVES EMOTIONALLY

Inviting ourselves emotionally means caring for our mental health by making appropriate choices in life. Leaders who have learned to handle stress and reduce anxiety in their own lives, and who are able to function in psychologically healthy ways, are in the best position to serve others.

Some pressure and anxiety are normal parts of human existence and serve useful functions. They shape our relations with other people and serve as a catalyst for creativity and innovation. It is only when pressures build out of control that they cause distress.

Ways to be inviting to ourselves emotionally in the most difficult and frightening situations were provided by James B. Stockdale. In 1965, Vice Admiral (then Commander, USN) Stockdale was shot down over North Vietnam and was taken prisoner. He was released in 1972. During his long years of captivity he developed a philosophy of leadership. In speaking of the need for examples in personal leadership, he wrote: "Daily ritual seems essential to mental and spiritual health. I would do 400 pushups a day, even when I had leg irons on, and would feel guilty when I failed to do them. This ritual paid dividends in self-respect . . . (and) it also paid physical dividends."

Two aspects regarding the process of inviting ourselves emotionally are to share feelings and maintain a sense of humor. Thinking invitationally means to trust ourselves and others to the point where we can share emotions, including sadness and sorrow as well as happiness and joy. Not letting others share in our feelings can be as selfish as not caring about the feelings of others. In the long run, everybody comes out ahead when we express honest feelings in caring and appropriate ways.

Living an encapsulated existence without sharing any emotion may be safe, but it is suffocating. Silas Marner, in the book by the same title, represents the tragedy of living in a private world of nothingness. Silas found life so threatening that he retreated into himself, refusing to let any emotion escape. It was only through the love extended to him by his daughter Eppie that Silas was able to grow in trust of other human beings. Becoming an Invitational Leader requires that we work to share ourselves with others. We must never accept the commonly held myth that "it is lonely at the top." Indeed, as the pressures build, it becomes more important than ever to turn to those closest to us—those to whom we can talk in confidence with mutual respect and trust. In addition, the Invitational Leader must not take pride in stress, in reciting the litany of his or her responsibilities and obligations. It is all too easy to wear our "designer stress" for all to see, rather than dealing with it in a mature and reasonable manner.

Of course, being mature and reasonable should never preclude the opportunity to laugh at ourselves and the situations in which we find ourselves. Maintaining a sense of humor is critical when thinking invitationally. An example of a sense of humor, even in disinviting situations, was provided by the behavior of Arturo Toscanini, the great Italian conductor of the New York Symphony Orchestra. During a rehearsal, Toscanini flew into a tantrum with a player and ended by ordering the musician from the stage. As the musician reached the exit door he turned around and shouted: "Nuts to you!" Yelled back Toscanini, "It's too late to apologize!" As noted earlier, if we lose our sense of humor, we become dangerous to ourselves and dangerous to others.

Showing a sense of humor can sometimes ease the strain and give people a breather. Humor, when well-timed, can be the catalyst that moves conflicts towards resolution. Those who are not able to laugh may be in serious emotional trouble. To illustrate, there is the tale of a man who could not laugh. He consulted his doctor. After a careful physical examination of the man, the doctor pronounced, "There is nothing wrong with you physically. You need amusement. Go and hear the great comedian Grimaldi; he will make you laugh." Said the man, "I am Grimaldi." Humor is an affirmation of Invitational Leadership's cornerstones of respect, trust, optimism, and intentionality. Laughing at ourselves can do wonders for our own mental health; it can help to humanize us in the eyes of our associates; and it can encourage greater creativity and collaboration. Laugh whenever appropriate, for laughter is indeed like an invitation—it decreases social distance and invites relationships.

INVITING OURSELVES PHYSICALLY

Although it may seem self-evident, the ways leaders function are related to their physical health. Most people do not concern themselves about their health until they are in danger of losing it. It is the Invitational Leader's individual responsibility to maintain good health and avoid illness as much as possible.

Invitational Leadership is as demanding physically as it is emotionally and intellectually. It is vital to maintain proper physical health to cope with these demands. As Erick Fromm commented: "One's own person becomes an instrument in the practice of the art, and must be kept fit according to the specific functions it has to fulfill" (p. 8). Our obligation to be physically fit includes all the things we have been taught (but sometimes find hard to practice). These include restricting high-cholesterol foods and moderating consumption of sugar, salt, alcohol, and other substances that may impede healthy living. It also includes exercising regularly, eliminating smoking or other drugs that contribute to physical problems, undergoing regular medical and dental checkups, and finding ways to relax and enjoy life.

A healthy respect for our feelings is most useful in inviting ourselves physically. For example, if exercising at night after a hard day at the office seems terribly difficult, we might try exercising at lunchtime with a brisk walk, or exercising in the morning before breakfast. The goal is to negotiate with ourselves (the ever-present whispering self) so that the probability of a healthy physical self is enhanced. Although specific suggestions regarding healthy living are far too numerous to list here, there are countless books on the subject available at bookstores.

One additional comment on inviting ourselves physically is to give special attention to our physical appearance. Police officers, military personnel, medical professionals, business leaders, and others have long recognized the importance of their physical appearance in projecting an image of professionalism. For instance, few people would risk getting on a commercial airplane if the pilot and co-pilots were wearing tank-tops! Avoid drabness, stand tall, dress well, eat less, and live with a flourish. We may not always win, but we can look good losing.

INVITING OURSELVES INTELLECTUALLY

It has been said that "Smart is not something you are, smart is something you get." The best way to get smart is to be intellectually inviting with ourselves. One of the most exciting discoveries of modern times is the awareness that human capacity is vastly greater than anything ever before imagined. Intelligence is not fixed and development is not predetermined. Intelligence evolves according to beneficial or lethal internal and external conditions. Getting smart is something that happens by way of intellectual stimulation over a lifetime.

A second way to invite ourselves intellectually requires participation in a wide variety of activities that increase knowledge, sharpen thought processes, and improve the overall power of the mind. Boredom can be the number one enemy. It is vital to devise strategies to fight boredom. Reading extensively on a variety of subjects that may be distant from our professional interests; visiting museums, zoos, libraries, art and science exhibits; joining organizations, such as discussion groups and historical societies—these are simply the tip of the iceberg. We should also remember the words of Oscar Wilde: "When you're invited to a dinner party, you have a moral obligation to be interesting!" The more we can do to combat our own boredom, the more we will find ourselves helping to combat that of others.

An important third way to invite ourselves intellectually is to manage time wisely. As a student reminded the authors:

"Time management is actually 'me' management." There are exactly 86,400 seconds in each 24-hour day. We all get the same amount of time. Daily goals for the Invitational Leader would include such simple practices as going to bed early enough to allow ample sleep, arising in time for a leisurely breakfast, and observing rest periods, including a full lunch hour and perhaps a short afternoon break. We accomplish more, not less, when we manage our time properly, which includes taking time for ourselves.

Inviting ourselves intellectually is to recognize that everybody cannot do everything all the time. It is healthy to find our cruising speed and to recognize our limitations as well as our potentials. Being less than perfect requires courage. As Bertrand Russell warned: "One of the symptoms of an approaching nervous breakdown is the belief that one's work is terribly important." There are times when the best course of action is to "raise the drawbridge"—to ask the world to stand back so we can take a breather.

In inviting ourselves intellectually, it is also necessary to welcome change. Change is the only constant in life. Everything changes, including mountains, rivers, and oceans. Life is a journey, not a destination. As Bill Stafford, a valued colleague, explained: "How we conduct ourselves on this journey is the whole meaning of our lives. Our destination can be understood only in these terms."

We recall a quote by Omar Kayyam: "The moving finger writes, and having writ, moves on. Not all your piety and wit can lure it back to cancel half a line, nor all your tears wash out a word of it." Invitational Leaders accept change, particularly change in positive directions. For example, it is better to be healthy rather than unhealthy, stable rather than unstable, flexible rather than rigid, therapeutic rather than lethal, and decent rather than indecent. Invitational Leaders accept change and roll with the punches of life.

Few writers have expressed the importance of being intellectually inviting with ourselves as well as Martin Gill: "I am prepared to add what follows, that since everything ends badly for us, in the inescapable catastrophe of death, it seems obvious that the first rule of life is to have a good time; and the second rule is to hurt as few people as possible in the course of doing so. There is no third rule." By being personally inviting with ourselves psychologically, physically, and intellectually, Invitational Leaders serve as powerful role-models for others.

INVITING OURSELVES SEMANTICALLY

It is difficult to sustain the effort required to be an Invitational Leader if we are beleaguered by undisciplined internal dialogue. The way to confront and change faulty and counter-productive inner whispers is to be aware of illusions caused by "tunnel vision," focusing on a few aspects of a situation while missing, ignoring, excluding, or distorting other relevant information.

We are most likely to change faulty internal dialogue when we become aware that information represents an anomaly with respect to existing self-talk, that this information should fit with existing beliefs, and that this reconciliation is impossible. The result is that the individual seeks to reduce tension by changing the internal world to accommodate new information.

The following are forms of irrational thinking and their cures. We have taken the liberty of naming these cures "Invitational Remedies." Here are some irrational thoughts along with their invitational antidotes.

BLACK OR WHITE THINKING (DICHOTOMOUS REASONING).

There is only one answer and only one way of looking at things: "I am either a total success or a total failure." In this all-or-nothing mental universe, there is no middle ground. Anything less than perfect is flawed: "People are either with me or against me, either friend or enemy, either adore me or hate me." Categories used by those who practice black or white thinking include "never-always," "everybody-nobody," "winners-losers," "all-nothing," "perfect-terrible," "success-failure," "victory-defeat." These individuals live in a dichotomous world of polar opposites. Anything less than one hundred percent is zero.

INVITATIONAL REMEDY.

Think in terms of gray areas. Analyze situations in terms of percentages or time. Things are seldom 100 percent bad. Perhaps 10 percent, or 30 percent, but not totally bad. Regarding time, do we ever have a completely bad day? Perhaps a bad five minutes, or even a bad hour or two, but not an entire bad day. The goal of invitational thinking is to consider things in a more balanced way. Mistakes can be opportunities to learn. As Invitational Leaders we accept our virtues along with our faults.

In the television series Northern Exposure, an Eskimo remarks: "Maybe it does not matter which path we embark on—maybe what matters is that we embark. If you start down a path and get lost, turn back and go down a different path. You will learn from each path you embark on, right or wrong." This remark implies a profound question: "Did I try and fail, or did I fail to even try?" When we act and fail, we can use the experience to learn and develop. Thinking invitationally requires us to recognize our own strengths as well as our weaknesses, our potential as well as our limitations, and our successes as well as our failures.

MENTAL FILTERING.

Some individuals focus on a particular set of circumstances while overlooking or shrugging off all other data. "Why is it," asked a colleague, "that every time I do something good, I say to myself, 'Anybody could have done that as well as I or better.'" "And why is it," she continued, "that every time I do something bad, I say to myself, 'Nobody has done as badly as I.'" Words associated with mental filtering are "awful," "appalling," "alarming," "disturbing," "devastating," "catastrophic," "dreadful," "ghastly," "horrible," and simply "terrible." When such people smell flowers, they look around for a funeral.

INVITATIONAL REMEDY.

Look for evidence of the good things that have happened during the day, or think of the positive aspects of a situation to balance the negative. So-called problems can turn out to be opportunities, as well as vice versa.

There is a story about an old man and his young son who lived a destitute life in a poor village. The old man owned one horse he used to plow his fields. One day the horse ran away. "Bad luck," said the neighbors. The old man replied, "Bad luck, good luck, who can say?" A few days later the horse returned home, leading a herd of half-wild mares. This made the old man rich, and the neighbors shouted, "Good luck!" And the old man responded, "Good luck, bad luck, who can say?" During the next week the young son attempted to train the half-wild mares and was thrown, crippling him for life. "Bad luck!" cried the neighbors. Again, the old man said, "Good luck, bad luck, who can say?" A month later, an army marched through the village, conscripting all the able-bodied young men and marching them off to war, leaving the crippled young man behind. Once again the neighbors cried, "Good luck," and once again, the old man replied, "Good luck, bad luck, who can say?" Invitational Leaders keep an open mind regarding all aspects of a situation.

MIND READING.

It is easy to imagine that others are having thoughts or saying things that are simply nonexistent. One person says, "Good morning," and the second person thinks, "What did she mean by that remark?" or "She likes me!" It is risky to project our own feelings onto other people's behavior.

INVITATIONAL REMEDY.

Believing that we can know what others are thinking is risky until we have checked out our assumptions in plain language. We illustrate the value of verification with a brief story: A local politician disliked having his wife attend political rallies because she always seemed to frown when he was on the stage speaking. This was most disconcerting to the politician. When he finally asked his wife about the frowns, she explained that she was totally unaware of her facial expressions. A trip to the optometrist revealed that she was near-sighted. She had been frowning to focus her distance vision. All of us misread signs at one time or another, perhaps reflecting our own self-doubts and uncertainties. As with so much else in the life, such doubts can often be remedied by simple communication: Ask for verification.

CATASTROPHIZING.

Examples of this type of irrational thinking would be an unsure public speaker who whispers to herself as she is being introduced: "What if my mind goes blank? What if I faint? What if the audience walks out on me? What if I lose my notes?" The list of worst possible scenarios is endless. By focusing on the negative things that could happen, we confuse fantasy with reality, and we risk becoming too cautious in our behavior. That's not the kind of risk an Invitational Leader should be taking; instead, he or she should be a boundary monitor, an explorer, a lifelong learner, able to envision positive yet realistic scenarios for the future. It is only by taking well-reasoned personal and professional risks, after all, that we manage to move from success as leaders to true significance.

INVITATIONAL REMEDY.

To counter the tendency toward catastrophizing, we

need to monitor carefully what we say to ourselves to challenge distorted assumptions, and also consider realistically the likelihood of a catastrophic event actually occurring. Again, we should check the facts. By challenging a self-debasing and self-destructive whispering self, we can alter irrational thoughts.

Being personally inviting with ourselves requires the separation of "good whispers" from "bad whispers" in our constant inner conversations. Compare the following lists, and imagine the resulting behaviors these whispers would generate:

Good Whispers	Bad Whispers
I have good friends.	I'm not close to anyone.
I am a friendly person.	I'm too shy to make friends.
I can make a difference.	There's nothing I can do.
I'll try something different.	Nothing works for me.
I prefer to be polite.	I must be polite.
I can handle things.	I've completely lost control.
I'm making progress.	I'll never finish.
I'll give it a try.	It won't work.
I'm pretty lucky.	I never win anything.

These positive and negative whispers are only examples of the countless ways that the inner voice can be our best friend or worst enemy.

It is clear that the whispering self can be managed by practicing a language of optimism. In the lexicon of an Invitational Leader's whispering self, "problem" becomes "situation," "lost" becomes "misplaced," "never" becomes "rarely," "can't" becomes "won't," "must" becomes "may," "always" becomes "often," and "need" becomes "want." Extending the language of optimism further, "elderly" becomes "older adults," "broken home" becomes "single parent family," "subordinates" becomes "associates," "sexual preference" becomes "sexual orientation," "physically handicapped" becomes "physically challenged," and "Orientals" becomes "Asians." As an Asian student said in correcting one of the authors: "Dr. Purkey, Oriental is a rug!"

Controlling what we say to ourselves involves a five-step process:

1. Bring the whispering self to a high level of awareness so that it is clearly recognizable.
2. Identify faulty, illogical, self-defeating, internal dialogue.
3. Challenge it.
4. Replace negative self-talk with positive and realistic thoughts.
5. Practice these positive and realistic thoughts until they become habit.

Being aware of and controlling internal conversations can make the difference between success or failure as an Invitational Leader.

THE WELL-ROUNDED LIFE

Much of what we've discussed in this chapter is a guide to developing a full and enriching personal life. As we have said before, the key for successful Invitational Leadership is keeping a balance between professional and personal concerns. Often there is no clear demarcation between the two, as ideally the Invitational Leader will be pursuing a life's work that has deeply personal significance. We might take as our model the invitational educator, someone whose passion for teaching and learning is inextricably tied to his or her passion for life. For such a fortunate person, what goes on in the classroom is merely one manifestation of a life dedicated to exploring fundamental questions and ideas.

Imagine, for instance, the literature professor teaching the close of Saul Bellow's novel *Mr. Sammler's Planet* (1970). The main character sits at the deathbed of a lifelong friend and quietly speaks a prayer, asking God to watch over the soul of his friend, someone who met at all costs the "terms of his contract, the terms which, in his inmost heart, each man knows. As I know mine. As all know. For that is the truth of it—that we all know, God, that we know, that we know, we know, we know" (p. 313). What inspiration might the professor find in talking over this scene with his or her class? What kind of personal significance might it have? Class over, the semester coming to a close, the professor might just reexamine his or her personal relationships and responsibilities, reassess past successes and failures, and make a renewed commitment to living a more impassioned existence.

We cite this passage from Saul Bellow and offer the attendant scenario because of its broader implications for Invitational Leadership. The corporate CEO or not-for-profit administrator might not be reading *Mr. Sammler's Planet*, it's true, but each of them might be making a more determined effort to cultivate all aspects of life—the psychological, the intellectual, the physical. They might be taking significant time away from the daily grind to enrich their marriages and family lives. They might be setting aside twenty minutes each evening to follow Covey's suggestion "to be alone and to think deeply, . . . reflect, write, listen, plan, visualize, ponder, relax." In so doing, they will be meeting the terms of a contract—not an employment or business contract — but the far more valuable and significant human contract, caring for themselves so they might care more completely for others — *inviting themselves personally* so that they might offer the same invitation to others.

CHAPTER SEVEN:
INVITING OTHERS PERSONALLY

*The truth of relationships, however, return in the rediscovery of con-
nection. In the realization that self and other are interdependent, and
that life, however valuable in itself, can only be sustained by care in
relationships.*

Carol Gilligan, *In a Different Voice* (1982, p. 127)

As we made clear at the close of chapter six, the importance
of inviting ourselves personally has implications far beyond
mere personal satisfaction or happiness. To invite ourselves
personally helps us to establish health of mind and body, as well
as emotional and spiritual health. From this position we are
better able to turn toward others with empathy and respect,
inviting those closest to us to realize their full potential.
Inviting ourselves personally, then, is one of the cornerstones of
sound leadership precisely because it allows us to invite *others*
personally. Our families, friends, and colleagues deserve nothing less than our full respect and trust. We must practice the art
of intentionality in each and every interaction, making it our
purpose to free others to do what Joseph Campbell so beautifully defines as "finding [their] bliss."

151

Invitational Leaders require the nurturing of fellow human beings and the giving of nurturing in return. A major source of nurturing is to love and be loved—something that is essential to our lives. Being in love is a highly inspiriting process. It is only with our human life support systems that we can develop optimally.

E. E. Cummings (1991) captures this point perfectly in two cogent sentences: "We do not believe in ourselves until someone reveals that deep inside us something is valuable, worth listening to, worthy of our trust, sacred to our touch. Once we believe in ourselves we can risk curiosity, wonder, spontaneous delight, or any experience that reveals the human spirit." We can never escape the fact that there are those relatives, lovers, friends, and associates whose lives are within our influence. Many of us do not realize our relatively boundless potential until someone sends us the right invitation.

The greatest life support systems are relatives, friends, colleagues, and lovers. This is why inviting others personally plays such an important role in becoming an Invitational Leader. Professional success, no matter how great or in what area, cannot make up for lack of success in personal relationships. Even a single invitation has the potential of influencing the course of another person's life.

Here is how Abraham Maslow (1954) explained the power of human relationships: "Let people realize that every time they threaten someone or humiliate or hurt unnecessarily or dominate or reject another human being, they become forces for the creation of psychopathology, even if these be small forces. Let them recognize that every man who is kind, helpful, decent psychologically, democratic, affectionate, and warm, is a psycho-therapeutic force even though a small one" (p. 254). In a very real way, we create one another, for good or ill.

MAKING CHOICES

Invitations are not accidents, they are choices. We choose to invite or not invite, to accept or not accept, invitations. These choices, large and small, are critical. Even the smallest has boundless potential. They may be overlooked, but they are always significant. The smallest invitation may be the beginning of the greatest opportunity.

Interacting with other people involves four basic choices: "sending," "not sending," "accepting," and "not accepting." To think invitationally is to recognize the dynamic interactions and relationships that exist among these four choices. Recognizing that we have the power and responsibility to make significant choices is central to Invitational Leadership. Our moral character as leaders is determined by the invitations we choose to send or not send, accept or not accept.

By analogy, these choices can be visualized as push buttons on a communication system. In every human interaction these decisions determine the quality of our lives.

The value and beauty of making choices in life is reflected in Homer's *Odyssey*. In this monumental story, Ulysses meets Calypso, who is immortal. She is fascinated by Ulysses and even envies him because he will not live forever. His life somehow becomes more vibrant, fuller, every decision is more significant, because his time on earth is limited. What he chooses to do represents real choice and real risk. The Invitational Leader's first decision is in sending invitations.

SENDING

Each of us decides what invitations we will send to others. This decision gives us great power, for we are an essential part of those opportunities others have for acceptance. When two or more people interact, an open system is created which has a life of its own. The behavior of either person acts as both cause and effect on the other. This "circular causality" transcends the behavior of either person, and contains risks as well as promises.

Sending any invitation inevitably contains risks. When we invite others to join with us in any human activity we risk being misunderstood or having the invitation rejected. Even having an invitation accepted is risky, for that, too, carries responsibilities. Yet, to be a leader it is essential to invite. Invitational Leaders take the attitude that risks are to be taken and not avoided. All the beautiful intentions in the world will not add up to a single inviting act. They mean little if they are not manifested in action.

It is within our power to determine the quality and quantity of the invitations we send. To illustrate, one of the authors had a co-worker of disinviting disposition. (Colleagues swear he must live under a bridge, like Billy Goat Gruff.) Each morning I passed Billy's office and wished him a good morning. Billy only growled in response. One day a colleague asked me why I continued to say good morning to Billy, when he never responded in kind. I explained that I would not give Billy too much power. *When we only react to the behavior of others, we are being controlled by their actions.*

Perhaps the greatest risk in sending invitations is the fear of being rejected. This fear is often expressed by members of "Parents without Partners," who report that they do not extend invitations to potential partners for fear of being turned down. They possess whispering voices that cautions against risks. Yet the greatest hazard in life is to risk nothing, send nothing, accept nothing, be nothing. As a colleague suggested: "It's better to invite and be rejected, than not to invite and be dejected."

As a reminder, a principle of Invitational Leadership is trust. Having trust in ourselves provides the courage to send invitations. It is also based on the principle of optimism regarding acceptance. When we have full confidence in an invitation being accepted, it usually is. This confidence, manifested in our trusting behavior, is likely to create the facts that prove the optimistic hypothesis to be true.

Leaders are sometimes indecisive about whether or not to become involved in situations. In Invitational Leadership, where respect, trust, optimism, and intentionality are anchoring points, taking risks is part of the job. There are times when it is necessary to make commitments and give our word that certain things will take place. Giving our word that something will happen *in advance of guaranteed proof* gives us the momentum to do what it takes to make the commitment come true. In life we pay full price for making dreams come true, and this payment is always paid in advance.

When the evidence for sending or not sending is about equally split, it is better to send. Few things in life are as sad as a missed opportunity. When an invitation is extended, there is no guarantee that it will be accepted. However, if an invitation is not extended, there is the absolute guarantee and assurance that it will not be accepted, no matter how beneficial the invitation might be. The rule is *Don't decide in advance about whether or not an invitation will be accepted.* Give the other person the opportunity to choose.

Some leaders have been known to justify their failure to invite by blaming their failure on others: "She never invites me, so why should I invite her?" Using the failure of others to be inviting is no excuse for our own failure to invite. Excuses do not free us from our responsibilities as Invitational Leaders.

An illustration of indecisiveness and vagueness in

extending invitations was provided by a couple's interaction during a marriage counseling session conducted by one of the authors. During the session the husband stated, "I always ask you to make love but you never say yes." The wife responded, "How do you ask?" And the husband responded, "I say I'm going to go upstairs and take a hot bath." His wife looked at him incredulously and gasped, "And that's what you meant?!?" Some invitations are never accepted because they are never received. Messages get lost, notes are misfiled, comments go unheard, questions remain unanswered, phone, e-mail, and fax messages are misdirected, and gestures escape notice. There are countless examples of messages sent but never received. Invitations are like letters: they sometimes get lost in the mail.

Because messages can be misdirected or misunderstood, it is vital that the leader ensure that messages are received and acted upon. This is clearly the leader's responsibility. When an invitation is sent but not received, or received but not understood, the leader may mistakenly assume that the invitation has been received. These breakdowns in communication can be avoided if the leader insures that accurate reception has occurred.

In the military services, the receiver of a communication is required to acknowledge and repeat the message verbatim before it is considered sent. To illustrate, the captain of a ship sends the message to the helmsman: "Four degrees port." The helmsman responds: "Aye, aye, Captain, four degrees port." A good rule of thumb is to request that messages are recognized, understood, and acknowledged by those who are expected to put them into action. There are dangers in making assumptions. As Carl von Clausewitz, the great authority on military tactics, warned, the fog of war is thick even in the most advantageous or routine circumstances. *Assumptions are never made if there are any means possible for verification.*

Another example may be found in aircraft navigational control systems. As an aircraft goes from one ground controller to another, the pilot "checks in" and identifies his or her aircraft, altitude, and direction of flight. Identification, altitude, and direction must be acknowledged by both parties, in the air and on the ground, to insure the safety of the aircraft.

The likelihood that a leader's invitations will be accepted is increased when the message is explicit. While there are dangers in being too explicit, which could lead to rudeness or coming on too strong, the advantages of sending clear and unmistakable messages are obvious. A classic illustration of directness was provided by Sir Winston Churchill in his first statement as Prime Minister to the House of Commons on May 12, 1940: "I have nothing to offer but blood, toil, tears, and sweat." Churchill made certain that his clarion call of greatness to the British People was unambiguous.

One of the great values in sending invitations is that we offer others options and choices. If we invite, others may accept. If we don't invite, they cannot accept. At heart, human beings have a deep longing to be invited to realize their potential. Many of us lie awake at night with a feeling that we should be somewhere, and yet we do not know where that place might be. This is a sign of a deeper yearning to realize our boundless potential in all areas of human endeavor. This potential can only be realized through the facilitation of others. Emerson expressed it this way: "We mark with light in the memory the few interviews we have had, in the dreary years of routine and of sin, with souls that made our souls wiser; that spoke what we thought, that told us what we knew; that gave us leave to be what we only were." It is only through the invitations extended to us by others that we have the opportunity to make choices and develop optimally. Opportunities are everywhere, but little happens without invitations being sent, received, and acted upon.

NOT SENDING

It may seem paradoxical, but sometimes the most inviting thing an Invitational Leader can do is not to invite. If an associate is trying to lose weight, we should not encourage him or her to eat more food. If someone is trying to quit smoking, we don't offer a cigarette. If a friend has a problem with alcohol, we don't encourage that person to have a drink. There are times when it is both uncaring and inappropriate to send an invitation.

It has been said that a good way to fail is to do a good job at the wrong thing. An equally good way to fail is to do a good job on something that should not be done at all. In some situations, doing and saying nothing may be the best thing an Invitational Leader can do. For example, rushing in to assist an associate on a task that is well within the power of the associate to handle may reflect lack of trust or respect. Thinking invitationally might be as simple as knowing precisely when to leave people alone.

As we've seen, not sending invitations has its own serious drawbacks. The unwillingness to invite can be as lethal as the willingness to disinvite. Every invitation we send, no matter how small or in what area, has limitless potential. We often overlook or underestimate this potential because the impact of an invitation may not be evident for weeks, months, or even years later. The stone mason may strike the stone a hundred times before the stone splits, yet each strike counts. Even the smallest invitation can have a far-reaching impact. And even if some invitations are never accepted, we may have made it easier for some future invitations to be accepted. Failing to act usually profits us little. If we invite, others may accept; if we don't, they can't.

ACCEPTING

Although we have relatively boundless potential in all areas of human endeavor, the realization of this potential is limited by time and circumstance. Thus, a critical ingredient in life is our ability to make choices to accept or reject what it offers.

An acceptable invitation requires a match between the sender's intentions and the receiver's perceptions. We are more likely to accept invitations when we see the sender as trustworthy and the invitation as beneficial. When an invitation is accepted and good things result, it increases the likelihood that future invitations will be accepted. Conversely, when an invitation is accepted and bad things result, it increases the likelihood that future invitations will be rejected. It is vital that the Invitational Leader not only send caring and appropriate invitations, but also that he or she works to insure that others have a reasonable chance of accepting and acting on them successfully.

The invitations we send are most likely to be accepted when they are specific enough to be understood, appropriate to the situation, and are seen as caring and respectful. They should not be overly-demanding. A colleague, Bruce Voelkel, pointed out the value of a "limited time" invitation. An example would be explaining to an unexpected visitor, "I have to attend a meeting in fifteen minutes, but meanwhile, let's go have a cup of coffee and talk." Such an invitation lets both parties know that they do not have to invest a great deal of time, and thus makes the invitation easier to extend and accept.

Some leaders have difficulty in accepting invitations because of a whispering self that murmurs that he or she is not deserving, that the invitation is not sincere, or that accepting is too risky. Yet accepting an invitation can be a most caring and appropriate act. In fact, accepting can be a form of giving. To illustrate, in some parts of the world the gracious thing to do is to thank a beggar for accepting our coin. Through the beggar's acceptance of the coin, we are allowed to be generous.

Accepting an invitation is another way of saying "I trust myself, I trust you, I trust life." Tom Robbins (1976), in his book *Even Cowgirls Get the Blues*, introduces a young woman who has very large thumbs and who loves to hitch-hike. In describing the young woman's large thumbs, Robbins writes: "They were not a handicap. Rather, they were an invitation, a privilege audaciously and impolitely granted, perfumed with danger and surprise, offering her greater freedom of movement, inviting her to live life at some 'other' level" (p. 51). A great tragedy in life is not having the courage to accept what life offers.

NOT ACCEPTING

Having stated the importance of sending, not sending, and accepting invitations, it is necessary to note that not accepting can also be a most caring and appropriate action. It is folly to think that all opportunities should be seized, and it would be folly to do so. Knowing when not to accept an invitation is an essential part of Invitational Leadership. An example of caring and appropriate behavior in not accepting an invitation would be at a party where the host encourages us to stay longer, even though it is obvious that the host is tired. At such a time, the most gracious thing to do is to decline the offer and head for the door.

As with the other possibilities, not accepting involves risks, perhaps the greatest risks of all. People who continuously reject invitations risk the possibility of living lonely, isolated, empty lives. Henry James wrote a story about a man who had a nagging suspicion that something terrible was going to happen to him during his life. He worried constantly about it. When he reached middle age, he figured out what the terrible thing was going to be. The terrible thing was that absolutely nothing was going to happen to him! He was going to go

through his entire life safely, without adventure, without sending, receiving, or accepting what life offers. By the time he figured it out, it was too late.

An illustration of the importance of invitations, even
when they are not accepted, was provided by Darryl Zanack,
the early Hollywood producer, in discussing his retirement:
"One thing I won't do is sit in Santa Monica and read in the
Hollywood Reporter about what goes on and wonder why I
wasn't invited to parties. I don't accept invitations now, but I
do receive them, and I don't want to know how it is not to be
invited anymore." To be treated as though one does not exist
can be a terrifying experience. We seem to have an innate
propensity to get ourselves noticed, and noticed favorably, by
others. To find ourselves in a society that does not even recognize our existence would be a horrible experience. As the wife
of Willie Loman exclaimed in the play *Death of a Salesman*,
"Some attention must be paid this man!" When people are
treated as having no existence, they are likely to despair.

Leaders who think invitationally continue to be optimistic when facing rejection. Just because some invitations are
rejected does not mean that all will be or that the invitation was
worthless. Some invitations are rejected because the individual
feels that he or she is unable to meet the expectations of the
inviter, or that the invitation was insincere. At other times,
rejection may be caused by the tentative way the invitation is
extended: "We would love to have you join us, *if* you would
like to come." Invitations are far less likely to be accepted
when they appear to be unclear, uncertain, or uncaring.
Conditional invitations elicit conditional acceptance.

In some circumstances, declining an invitation may be
an acceptance in disguised form. In parts of the southern
United States, it is polite to decline an invitation the first time
to see if it is sincere. If the invitation is re-extended, then it is
accepted. It goes like this: "John, we would like you to come
with us to the concert on Wednesday evening." John responds:
"No, thanks, I don't want to impose." We reply: "You won't

be imposing, we really would like for you to come with us." So John says, "Well, O.K., if you're sure I won't impose." Declining the initial invitation may be a way of testing its sincerity.

An illustration of how accepting and rejecting invitations can be a confusing process was provided by a colleague. One of the authors invited a rather shy and private colleague to join him and his family for a holiday dinner. The colleague did not accept the invitation, even though he was assured that his presence at the dinner would be most welcome. On the evening of the dinner the colleague appeared at the doorway, totally unexpectedly. When he sensed the puzzlement of the hosts, he explained, "Well, I didn't say that I wasn't coming." To think invitationally is to keep in mind that non-acceptance is not the same as rejection.

This brings us once again to the importance of intentionality in Invitational Leadership. Awareness of how and when to invite, and how and when to accept and reject, are all parts of becoming an Invitational Leader. To be inviting even when others may be disinviting is the hallmark of Invitational Leadership.

In every interaction, we have this crucial choice set before us—to be inviting or to be disinviting. To choose to be inviting requires that we take risks by bringing the best parts of ourselves to bear on our relationships. To do any less is to fail our responsibilities as leaders and as human beings. Clearly we will fail at times, as all humans do, but it is the willful effort to move beyond complacency that distinguishes the invitational leader from others. We must make an abiding commitment to something bigger than what Walker Percy (1980) calls the "two percent self."

Will Barrett, Percy's main character in *The Second Coming*, hits upon this idea of the "two percent self" in the most unlikely of circumstances:

There at any rate stands Will Barrett on the edge of a gorge in old Carolina, a talented agreeable wealthy man living in as pleasant an environment as one can imagine and yet who is thinking of putting a bullet in his brain.

Fifteen minutes later he is sitting in his Mercedes in a five-car garage, sniffing the Luger and watching a cat lying in a swatch of sunlight under the rear bumper of his wife's Rolls-Royce Silver Cloud three spaces away. . . .

As he sat gazing at the cat, he saw all at once what had gone wrong, wrong with people, with him, not with the cat—saw it with the same smiling certitude with which Einstein is said to have hit upon his famous theory in the act of boarding a streetcar in Zurich.

There was the cat. Sitting there in the sun with its needs satisfied . . . the cat was exactly a hundred percent cat. No more, no less. As for Will Barrett, as for people nowadays—they were never a hundred percent themselves . . . . More likely they were forty-seven percent themselves or rarely, as in the case of Einstein on the streetcar, three hundred percent. All too often these days they were two percent themselves, specters who hardly occupied a place at all. How can the great suck of self ever hope to be a fat cat dozing in the sun?

There was his diagnosis then. A person nowadays is two percent himself. And to arrive at a diagnosis is already to have anticipated the cure: how to restore the ninety-eight percent? (pp. 13-15)

To go through life with only a tenuous connection to one's friends and family members, as well as one's business associates, is to live an impoverished existence. As Percy makes clear, the danger of such complacency is that we will become "specters who hardly occupy a place at all." To occupy a place fully means dedicating ourselves to others, inviting them personally, sending and receiving invitations in good faith. One possible cure for restoring the missing ninety-eight percent might very well be something akin to the model of Invitational Leadership, whereby we build mutually sustaining personal and professional relationships.

DEMONSTRATING RESPECT

An important aspect of inviting others personally is to maintain respect for other human beings. Hyams (1979), in his book *Zen and the Martial Arts*, gives an example of how apparent lack of respect was handled by a Japanese Zen Master. He was visited by a university professor who came to inquire about Zen. It was obvious to the Master from the start of the conversation that the professor was not so much interested in learning about Zen as he was in impressing the Master with his own opinions and knowledge. The Master listened and finally suggested they have tea. The Master poured his visitor's cup full and then kept on pouring. The professor watched the cup overflowing until he could no longer restrain himself: "The cup is over-full, no more will go in!" The Master replied, "Like this cup, you are full of your own opinions and speculations. How can I show you Zen unless you first empty your cup?" Those of us who practice Invitational Leadership demonstrate respect by "emptying our cups" when interacting with others.

Behaviors and comments that are perceived by others as condescending or demeaning are usually interpreted as disinviting regardless of one's intentions. Kidding others about their physical appearance, behavior, background, or misfortunes can be very disinviting. Saying "I was only kidding" is insufficient to repair the damage of a cruel jest. As a friend commented: "Sticks and stones may break my bones, but words will surely kill me."

Curiously, "inviting" and "disinviting" are often simultaneous processes. Saying something nice to a person, but using a sarcastic tone of voice, would be an example of this. Sarcasm is dirty fighting. What we are saying may be inviting, but how we are saying it may cause it to be very disinviting. Because this is so, to think invitationally is to develop sensitivity regarding how our words and actions are being perceived by other people.

The ability to sense what others are feeling is a special aim of Invitational Leadership. Because forming a bridge of understanding is so essential, leaders use *all* their senses in reading situations. An example of reading situations was provided by a Moroccan waiter who approached one of the authors and his spouse in a small restaurant in Tangiers and inquired about America. When the waiter was asked how he knew that we were American, he replied, "Americans smell different." Attending to sights, smells, sounds, and even touch are valuable skills for the Invitational Leader to acquire.

CULTIVATING FRIENDSHIPS

As noted earlier, giving attention to friends is essential. Through sharing the company of others, and through countless inviting actions, friendships are established and maintained. Friendships are also transferable. Friends of friends can become our friends. To illustrate, the spouse of one of the authors called her friend and invited her to go strawberry picking. The friend was not free to go, but suggested that one of her friends be asked. The result was that the invitation was extended and a new friendship was formed. Making and keeping friends allows us to think that we are able, valuable, and responsible, and that we are respected and worthy of trust.

Friendships are like gardens. They must be cultivated and nourished, even under the pressures of time and responsibilities. Recognizing birthdays, planning holidays together, and being there for the turning points of life, like christenings, graduations, anniversaries, weddings, retirements, and funerals are among the countless ways to let friends know that they are important to us. As Antoine De Saint-Exupery (1943) reminded us in *The Little Prince*, "To forget a friend is sad—not everyone has a friend" (p. 18). Invitational Leaders give friendships a high priority.

There are many forms of friendships. Some are casual and temporary, while others are deep and long-lasting relationships. Both are part of a fulfilled life. It should be recognized, however, that friendships, as with all human interactions, can be either beneficial or destructive. Sometimes friends can be destructive by tempting or coercing others into unethical or personally injurious behaviors. Offering an alcoholic beverage to a friend with a serious drinking problem, or smoking around an acquaintance who is trying to break the habit, are examples of this. Conversely, positive friendships are the springboard for mutual support which summons people to face challenges and overcome barriers. The slogan "Friends don't let friends drive drunk" describes the result of beneficial friendships. We cannot fully experience life and successfully cope with its many difficulties without the benefits of friendships.

By definition, an invitation is a purposive and generous act. It is intended to offer something beneficial for consideration. There are few acts as generous and purposeful as an invitation to friendship. It is vital to cultivate and treasure a circle of trusted friends as well as to seek out new relationships and explore fresh interests.

Our friendships, if undertaken in the spirit of the invitational philosophy, will bolster our own leadership efforts, along with those of our friends. In other words, the invitations we send to our friends not only allow us to grow as individuals through their support, but they also give our friends the opportunity to grow through our faith in them. As Henry David Thoreau writes, "[Friends] cherish each other's hopes. They are kind to each other's dreams." Surely one of the great joys of life is the mutually loving exchange between friends, as they offer one another comfort, care, and encouragement. The ideal friendship, in short, is a model of the invitational relationship, working together on projects—in this case, the friendship itself—of mutual benefit.

CULTIVATING FAMILY

As we discussed in chapter six, the leader who makes little time for personal life, ignoring the responsibilities of family, will most certainly reap what he or she sows. Unfortunately, our culture is full of stories about workaholic fathers who find upon retiring that they have missed out on the most joyous parts of their lives. They look around themselves to find that they are strangers in their lives, with very little to show for years and years of hard work at the office. Instead, they face the daunting prospect of jump-starting relationships they had formerly neglected.

One study in Pennsylvania reveals that spouses talk to each other an average of four minutes per day, and that parents talk to children an average of thirty seconds per day. This profound lack of communication does much to account for the behavior of the teenagers of Georgia's Rockdale County, which was the focus of a recent *Frontline* special. Returning to empty houses after school, many of these children gathered to drink alcohol, smoke marijuana, and often had indiscriminate sexual encounters. An unusually high number of gonorrhea cases tipped off medical and social workers that something was amiss in their community. Needless to say, the parents were aghast, yet they seemed unwilling to accept their share of the responsibility for this behavior. Parent after parent replied that they had recognized nothing seriously wrong, that the family had seemed fine, fairly healthy. Several did admit, however, with the clarity of hindsight, that little substantial communication took place in their households.

How can we learn to recognize these problems before they envelop an entire community? The invitational model offers one possible solution, not as it applies to leadership but as it concerns the whole person. If Invitational Leadership is defined by the values of trust, respect, optimism, and intentionality, then the invitational person—the *whole* person—can be recognized by the extent to which those values carry over into his or her personal life. Family life, perhaps above all, must be the central arena for the sending and receiving of invitations. Indeed, if we cannot muster enough enthusiasm to engage fully in the lives of those closest to us, then surely we have failed to meet the terms of our basic human contract. The invitational person wishes to see his or her family members realize their potential in all areas of human endeavor, recognizing that his or her own personal growth depends in large part on the strong support system provided by family. To realize our potential as family members is to do whatever is necessary to spend significant amounts of time in communication and communion with our loved ones.

CELEBRATING LIFE

The celebration of life is not simply the clamor and excitement of a Mardi Gras. It is a meaningful celebration of the deeper significance and richness of personal existence. More specifically, celebrating life is an intentional activity that contributes to a variety of developmental processes. Leaders who intentionally reach out to what life offers and invite others to do the same are most likely to develop friendships and celebrate life.

The value of reaching out was illustrated by a friend's story:

> Many years ago, when I was a child, I used to go and
> live with a farm family for a month-long summer

holiday. It was grand fun and filled with adventures: jumping in the hayloft, gathering eggs, trying to milk cows, and playing with the family's children. When I entered adolescence I stopped going to the farm, but I always remembered those golden summer days. Years later, when I was a college student, I wrote a letter to the father of the farm family to express how very much I enjoyed the family's hospitality. More years rolled by, then recently I encountered one of the farm family members. When I asked how everyone was, I was told that the father had died. The family member said: "I was hoping to run into you, for I want to share something. After our father died we went to the bank and opened his safety deposit box. There was not a lot there ... some old coins, deed to the farm, some legal papers... and the letter you had written to my father." We may never know how much a single thoughtful act can be so valuable in another person's life.

As with other aspects of life, celebration sometimes involves risks. Being personally inviting with others can be met with misunderstandings, suspicions, and rejection. It can be risky to say to a valued colleague, "I'm very fond of you" or "I appreciate you." Those who think invitationally understand these hazards and, through the principles of respect, trust, optimism, and intentionality, continue to reach out in caring and appropriate ways.

One of our students shared a celebration of life that is worth repeating here:

I want to tell you about something I saw in San Jose, California that was both funny and deeply moving. I was singing in an Italian restaurant-nightclub where there were three other singers, a pianist, and an accordionist who provided the entertainment. This consisted of operatic arias and Italian songs. The tenor was an Hungarian with a fantastic voice—as good as any Italian on records of operas. He could hit a high C note that gave people goose-bumps. He was a favorite of the clientele, and there was much applause, shouting, bravos, whistling, etc., after each of his arias. One night we had a new Italian cook in the kitchen—straight from Italy—who didn't even speak English. I shall never forget the way he looked when the tenor sang. He looked like he had just seen Jesus walk into the dining room. At the end of the aria, the cook, with great joy and tears, hugged the tenor and kissed him. It was a loud, happy, tearful, affectionate, funny, and very caring experience for all of us who were part of it. Everyone cried.

When a chance to celebrate life is offered, take the chance. There may not be another opportunity.

We must never lose sight of those things in life that truly matter. A personal story from one of the authors might help bring this abstract point to life:

Several years ago, my son and I were involved in a bad car accident. My son had been visiting from college and was preparing to return, and together we were making a quick trip to the bank to withdraw money for his trip. It was one of those rare winter days in Georgia, a gorgeous day. As we rode along, I said, "Michael, are you wearing your seatbelt?" He said, "No, I'm too tall; I don't like to wear it." I said, "You need to wear it. Start wearing your seatbelt." We entered the intersection, and I said to him, "Michael, this is the most dangerous intersection in our county." He said, "You're right, Mom; I can't see around the cars." We entered the intersection, and within ten seconds we were hit broadside by a truck. We were both knocked out. Our new car was totaled.

When I came to, every window in our car was smashed out, and Michael was lying in a sea of glass. Glass was in his hair, his mouth, his eyes—I thought he was dead. His face was covered with blood. I looked over at him and said, "Michael! Michael! Are you all right?" Finally, after a long moment, he opened his eyes and said, "Be cool, Mom; everybody is looking." I thought to myself that anybody who is worried about the way he looks must be all right. He was pinned in the car, but the minute I found him breathing and talking, I opened my door, jumped out, and began directing traffic! I was waving both arms and shouting, "Let's move it. Come on; let's keep moving."

Finally, after the longest delay, the solitary wail of the ambulance came, and they got Michael out of the car. As I walked with him to the ambulance, he reminded me to get his Christmas jacket out of the car. So I ran back to the car to get his coat and my briefcase, my albatross. When we got to the hospital, and they pulled Michael out of the ambulance, I got up to walk out and couldn't move. I had a broken foot, three broken ribs, a concussion, and lacerations from head to toe on one side. Why couldn't I get up now, when before I had moved about with ease? It was that immediately after the accident I had been concentrating on those riches in which I was truly wealthy. Everything else, even my own pain, did not register. I was absorbed in what truly matters, and the rest of the world faded from view. I resolved never to forget that moment.

As Invitational Leaders, all of us must learn to juggle a wide variety of duties. Like everyone else, we find ourselves juggling both rubber balls and glass balls. The rubber balls represent work and our place in our profession. Because these work balls bounce, when we drop one, it comes back to us and we can begin juggling again. But glass balls don't bounce. When we drop a glass ball, if it does not break, we must reach down and pick it up—it will not bounce back. If we are not so fortunate, it will shatter where it lands. These glass balls represent family and friends and health. Our message, then, is that we should show extraordinary care with these glass balls—family, friends, and health—because they truly are our most precious possessions.

THE NEXT STEP

One of the primary messages of Invitational Leadership is that the business of life is connectedness, whether we are discussing our personal or professional journeys. We issue invitations to ourselves and to others, hoping that we can find that common ground from which to reach new levels of significance. Indeed, Invitational Leadership is by definition a journey from success to significance, as we realize that our professional success is only meaningful within the context of personal happiness. It is this kind of significance—establishing deeply sustaining relationships with family and friends—that makes all else possible.

From this place of personal and professional significance, we are able to take the next step in our leadership odyssey, extending our commitments to the communities of which we are part. We will close our book with a careful examination of leadership as a vibrant form of public service, locating the ultimate leadership role in the work of the leader as servant.

Before we begin this final exploration, however, we should be reminded once more of the relationships that sustain us. In Delmore Schwartz's poem "Do the Others Speak of Me

Mockingly, Maliciously?" (1967) the speaker discovers that despite the risks involved in matters of the heart, there is no other path to fulfillment than that which runs through our complex, baffling, and yet joyous personal relationships:

> What an unheard-of thing it is, in fine,
> To love one another and equally be loved!
> . . . We need
> Each other's clumsiness, each other's wit,
> Each other's company and our own pride. I need
> My face unshamed, I need my wit, I cannot
> Turn away. We know our clumsiness,
> Our weakness, our necessities, we cannot
> Forget our pride, our faces, our common love. (pp.
> 69-70)

Connectedness, communication, collaboration—these are the values that motivate us in issuing our personal invitations to others. These are also the values at the core of public service. Even as this passage so movingly captures the "necessities" of personal life—the "company" of others who accept both our "weakness" and our "pride"—it also hints at larger connections, the "common love" that binds us together at the public level, as well. Public or private, personal or professional—the Invitational Leader will always go forward in a posture of empathy, respect, and service. The key is consistency of philosophy and character, as the Invitational Leader, inspired by the mutual support and care of family and friends, expands his or her work into the larger community.

CHAPTER EIGHT:
THE INVITATIONAL
LEADER AS SERVANT

It is high time that the ideal of success be replaced by the ideal of service.

—Albert Einstein

In 1983 Time magazine named the computer their Man of the Year. Even today, with technology such a central part of our everyday lives, this gesture seems astonishing. Did no person live enough, care enough, give enough to be named Man of the Year? Our choice that year would have been the man in the Potomac helping with the rescue after the crash of the Air Florida jet — the person Roger Rosenblatt wrote so movingly about as the "man in the water" (1982).

On the day of the crash, the wintry weather had caused ice to form on the jet's wings, and the plane hit the Potomac Bridge, crashed into the river, and quickly began to sink. A group of survivors huddled together on the tail of the plane to keep themselves above the chilly waters. Television cameras were on the scene immediately, and they picked up hovering helicopters dropping lifeline flotation rings, reminding us all of the reality of what happens to people when they are most vulnerable.

Time and again one brave survivor, without hesitation, caught the flotation ring and gave it to someone else. When the ring finally came down for the last time to rescue the man who had sacrificed himself to save all the others, he was so diminished in energy and so chilled by the icy water that he could not pull himself up. Instead he slid to death before our very eyes. The TV cameras had captured this ordinary man doing an extraordinary thing.

The scholar Joseph Campbell refers to the "hero with a thousand faces," implying that true heroism emerges from ordinary lives put to extraordinary tests. Any face you pass on the street might be, in dire circumstances, the face of an astonishingly brave and selfless hero. Of course, we need not have our lives threatened to discover something of the "hero with a thousand faces" within ourselves. Heroism can reveal itself in countless everyday actions, or in what the poet William Wordsworth refers to as our "little, nameless, unremembered acts / Of kindness and of love."

Consider the philosophy of Ezra, the cook in Anne Tyler's novel *Dinner at the Homesick Restaurant*:

> He cooked what people felt homesick for—tacos like those from vendors' carts in California, which the Mexican was always pining after; and that wonderful vinegary North Carolina barbeque that Todd Duckett had to have brought by his mother several times a year in cardboard cups. He would call it the Homesick Restaurant. (p.1)

By serving the food everyone "was pining after," Ezra was able to make dinner at his restaurant a moving experience, giving his customers a tangible sense of connection with their pasts. An ordinary act, but yet one that surely resonates strongly in the hearts and minds of the customers. It is this kind of everyday kindness that forms the best portion of our lives, and it is perhaps no exaggeration to say that these acts are merely a few small steps away from acts of courageous heroism. If we condition our hearts by performing kindnesses of the most ordinary variety, then surely we will prepare the ground for larger gestures of caring. It is hard to imagine that the man in the Potomac River, for instance, was not the author of a thousand previous "little, nameless, unremembered acts / Of kindness and of love."

The theory of Invitational Leadership is built upon the notion that it is precisely the "little, nameless" acts that reveal a leader's true character, inspire trust and respect among colleagues, and establish the foundation for a new kind of professional relationship based upon dialogue and collaboration. As we have shown throughout this book, the Invitational Leader begins his or her journey with what is closest to hand, turning within to answer the question "What is my meaning?" and inspiring family members, friends, and associates to do the same.

There is one more step, however, in this journey, and it is a crucial one. In pursuing more joyful and meaningful personal and professional lives, invitational leaders must consider their place within the larger community—for it is in service to community that the patterns of Invitational Leadership find their fullest expression. Just as the "hero with a thousand faces" may move from the smallest acts of kindness to larger gestures of selflessness, so the invitational leader may find that his or her capacity to serve others extends far beyond "ordinary" definitions of work and love. He or she may discover an astonishing capacity to be a steward of the public good—to be a servant, in the most ennobling sense of the word.

LEADERSHIP AS VIRTUE

At the close of chapter six, we referred to Saul Bellow's novel *Mr. Sammler's Planet*. In the final scene of that powerful novel, Mr. Sammler prays on behalf of his dying friend and in the process discovers an amazing truth about what he calls the "terms of [our] contract, the terms which, in his inmost heart, each man knows": "For that is the truth of it—that we all know, God, that we know, that we know, we know, we know." We repeat this quotation because we believe it captures something of the ethical foundation of Invitational Leadership. At the heart of this philosophy is the notion that we are ultimately responsible for treating others with respect and concern; indeed, intentionality—the quality of paying purposeful attention to our treatment of others—is one of the four principles of Invitational Leadership. Again, the Invitational Leader begins with what is closest to hand, developing an ethical system that will extend to his or her treatment of colleagues, family and friends, and further to the larger community.

One can find this basic ethical principle at the heart of many of the world's great moral systems. In discussing what it takes to lead a heroic life of the spirit, the late Reverend Frank Harrington (1993) discusses the "fundamental ingredient" of virtue:

> [Virtue] is the critical dimension that undergirds behavior. Real heroes are acting from a standpoint of virtue: honesty, honor, love, compassion, loyalty, responsibility, duty, sacrifice. These are the things that undergird heroic action—not self-aggrandizement, not ego satisfaction, not greed, anger, or intolerance. The greatest virtue of them all is to love your neighbor as you love yourself.

In Invitational Leadership, it is the movement from self-interest to selflessness and from exclusion to inclusion that marks the work of the best leaders. An important corollary of this is the Invitational Leader's ability to respond with empathy to other people, and to ask before making judgments how others might see things differently. As we noted in chapter four, partnerships and collaborations are far more likely to produce long-term positive results than open battles between competitors.

In another tradition, Confucian philosophy centers on a variation of the Golden Rule: "Do not impose on others what you yourself do not desire." In doing your best for others, Confucius implies, you should always proceed with empathy and respect, asking yourself what you would prefer were you in the other person's position. Living according to this principle, you gradually begin to make such decisions and judgments almost naturally, without excessive worry or sorrow. Thus, when Confucius says that at the age of seventy "I followed my heart's desire without stepping over the line," he clearly means that after a lifetime of following his own moral system, he is able to respond to situations with ease and grace. Importantly, the Confucian system makes no distinction between our behavior toward those closest to us and toward the community as a whole, insofar as its version of the Golden Rule is concerned.

We are reminded also of the famous words from Rabbi Hillel: "If I am not for myself, who will be for me? But if I am only for myself, what am I? And if not now, when?" Notice how these questions encapsulate an entire ethical philosophy: first there is the imperative need to turn within for the strength and sustenance of the inner life; second comes the acceptance of our responsibilities for others; and third comes the insistence that those responsibilities must be attended to here and now, in our everyday actions. It is an incisive reminder, in three brief questions, that we are indeed duty-bound to uphold the human contract.

Invitational Leadership rests upon a foundation of ethical commitment—one that follows from traditional sources of moral wisdom. As in each of the sources we have cited here, Invitational Leadership carries with it certain responsibilities beyond the immediate world of work and family. Just as our moral obligations govern our personal and professional lives— our roles as parents, partners, employees, colleagues—so, too, do they govern our lives in the communities of which we are part—our roles as citizens. When we speak of the Invitational Leader as servant, therefore, we are speaking of the leader as an engaged and purposeful citizen.

LEADERSHIP AS SERVICE

Perform random acts of kindness, or so the bumper sticker tells us. It is good advice, to be sure, calling for us to help tip the scales against the random acts of violence we hear recounted during the nightly newscast. Yet this simple imperative has much broader implications, for to be conscious of the possibility of performing acts of kindness is already to have changed our thinking. And a changed mind may lead in turn to changed behavior.

So random acts can become intentional acts. We prepare Thanksgiving dinner for an underprivileged family. We write a check to a favorite charity. Still, performing these activities, our impact, while positive, is limited. But what if we should volunteer to build a house with Habitat for Humanity? Or join an organization supplying medical relief to a third-world country? Doing these things, we are not acting alone, but rather in concert with others similarly given to acts of kindness. The scope and impact of our activity become much larger. In short, we are engaging in collaborative service. It is this level of commitment that Invitational Leaders can achieve within their organizations by placing service at the center of their mission.

Robert Greenleaf (2002) makes an eloquent case for the necessity of leaders to be concerned above all else with service:

> The servant-leader is servant first . . . . Becoming a servant leader begins with the natural feeling that one wants to serve, to serve first. Then conscious choice brings one to aspire to lead . . . . The best test, and the most difficult to administer, is this: Do those served grow as persons? Do they, while being served, become healthier, wiser, freer, more autonomous, more likely to become servants? (pp. 23-24)

There are two important implications for our purposes in Greenleaf's definition of the "servant-leader." First, by positing service as the prerequisite for inspired leadership, Greenleaf implies that leadership without service is something far less substantial—ego-driven rather than community-centered, selfish rather than empathetic. Invitational Leadership is firmly rooted in a philosophy of altruism and empathy, collaboration and cooperation.

Second, Greenleaf clearly believes that leadership involves teaching and mentoring, as one of the major requirements of leaders is that they invite others toward service. It is not enough that as Invitational Leaders we concern ourselves with organization and management; rather, our role is to inspire and instruct by example. Invitational Leadership assumes that one of the leader's most important duties is to lead by example, creating an atmosphere in which associates are summoned to realize their full potential as leaders themselves and, more generally, as human beings. Like Greenleaf, we believe that any individual's potential will ideally involve a commitment to serving others.

But, you may ask, what does service to community have to do with the work most people do at the office between nine and five? Everything, we would answer, especially if service is part of a full-scale institutional commitment. If the Invitational Leader is successful in directly and clearly communicating a mutually beneficial vision for a company or institution, and if he or she makes service or stewardship one of its prime values, then his or her associates at all levels will be made to feel that they are contributing to something much larger than themselves. As an example, we will use the field of higher education.

Administrators and faculty members at colleges and universities work in a field with a particular obligation to the larger community. Service is a natural part of a university's institutional mission—service toward students, on one level, and service on behalf of the future, on another, more abstract level. It is this second level of obligation that Anne Colby and Thomas Ehrlich (2000) discuss in *Civic Responsibility and Higher Education*. Their suggestions for universities seeking to have a more direct and concentrated role in preparing our communities for a better future capture something of our invitational model. Here is their first suggestion:

> A high degree of institutional intentionality in fostering moral and civic responsibility is the hallmark of those colleges and universities that lead in this arena. The campuses not only have mission statements that include this goal, but the statements are well known and understood by most students, faculty members, and staff. The administrative leadership speaks and acts in ways that promote the goal, as does faculty leadership. (p. xl)

This "high degree of intentionality" is a basic principle of Invitational Leadership, and Colby and Ehrlich define perfectly the reason for such intentionality—namely, so that the overall mission of the university will be well known at all levels of the institution. Further, Colby and Ehrlich insist that leaders themselves serve as inspiring examples, *both speaking and acting* in accordance with the institutional goals. This mixture of clear-sighted speech and intentional action is central to any Invitational Leader's success. As we have stated previously,

Invitational Leaders practice what they preach, convincing their associates that they have both a personal and professional stake in everyone's participation and welfare.

To return to Robert Greenleaf's words, the ultimate test of a servant leader's success is whether his or her associates and colleagues are more likely to become servants themselves as a result of that leader's influence. If leadership begins with a desire to serve others, part of its execution involves instilling these virtues at an institutional level, so that everything about the organization is built upon a shared sense of mission. The Invitational Leader, in education or any other field, intentionally creates a culture of collaborative service that will have implications far beyond daily assignments and meetings. What are these implications? They might be best captured in the simple wisdom of a bumper sticker, like the one with which we began this section: *Build a stronger community. Honor service. Perform collaborative acts of kindness.*

LEADERSHIP AS COMMUNITY-BUILDING

By creating a community in the workplace that represents the best of civic life, the Invitational Leader can have a profound effect on those who work within his or her organization. Not only does an inviting workplace provide an example of collaborative community building, it can also inspire employees to carry the organization culture and ethos into other aspects of their lives. Peter Block (1993) states the matter with admirable clarity in *Stewardship: Choosing Service Over Self-Interest*, as he implores us to become "part of creating something we care about":

> Let the commitment and the cause be the place where we work. It is not so much the product or service of our workplace that will draw us out of ourselves. It is the culture and texture and ways of cre-

ating community that attract our attention. Our task is to create organizations we believe in and to do it as an offering, not a demand. No one will do it for us. Others have brought us this far. The next step is ours. Our choice for service and community becomes the only practical answer to our concern about self-interest. (p. 10)

Block rightly points out that "the product or service of our workplace" is much less important than the pledge we make to create communities of which we can be proud. It must be intentional work, as well, the result of a deeply felt desire to serve others. Here our ethical commitments come together with our obligations as citizens; indeed, Invitational Leadership finds its fullest expression in this meeting. The leader as servant, collaborating with others to fulfill mutually beneficial goals, is ultimately a community-builder for the future.

Remember the lines that end Alfred Lord Tennyson's great poem "Ulysses"? He ends this dramatic monologue with Ulysses asking his comrades and friends to stay firmly on course by holding to their shared purpose to "seek a newer world":

It may be that the gulfs will wash us down:
It may be we shall touch the happy isles,
And see the great Achilles, whom we knew.
Though much is taken, much abides; and though
We are not now that strength which in old days
Moved earth and heaven, that which we are, we are:—
One equal temper of heroic hearts,
Made weak by time and fate, but strong in will
To strive, to seek, to find, and not to yield.

These lines hardly need our commentary, yet we do want to note the sense of risk, adventure, and sacrifice that attends the speaker's inspirational call. When Ulysses says, "That which we are, we are," the reader knows that what defines these men most precisely is their strength and desire. Despite all that might threaten their resolve, they will press on, for they have a shared vision—"One equal temper of heroic hearts"—made tangible by the stirring invitation their leader so memorably sends.

Perhaps it is making slight use of the poem to say that it presents the terms by which we can define the spirit of the Invitational Leader and the community he or she helps to build, but nevertheless it is inspiring to us for that reason. After all, as the beginning of this chapter makes clear, it does not take a Ulysses to perform heroically. Rather, the Invitational Leader is a "hero with a thousand faces," standing ready at all times to join in joyful work with other "heroic hearts."

LEADERSHIP AS ODYSSEY

We ended the first chapter of this book by recalling the questions Carl Sandburg asks in *Remembrance Rock*: "Who am I, and where have I been, and where am I going?" We added a fourth question, one for all Invitational Leaders—indeed, for everyone in every walk of life—to ask of themselves: "What is my meaning?" The lifetime journey of Invitational Leadership will allow us to answer that question in many different ways, but it always begins the same way: with that first crucial invitation we send to ourselves to begin the process of discovery.

This journey is marked at every stage by a general optimism about what we can accomplish. Though our optimism should be tempered with a realistic sense of the world and our place in it, it nevertheless should emerge as a natural expression of our leadership style. There is no doubt that Invitational Leadership requires a philosophical frame of mind. It encourages the kind of philosophical reckoning that is the happy product of the truly well-lived life. We end this final chapter by citing a poem that offers moving advice for the person seeking to live such a life. Here are the closing stanzas of Cavafy's "Ithaka" (1972):

> Hope the voyage is a long one.
> May there be many a summer morning when,
> with what pleasure, what joy,
> you come into harbors seen for the first time . . . .
> Keep Ithaka always in your mind.
> Arriving there is what you are destined for.
> But do not hurry the journey at all.
> Better if it lasts for years,
> so you are old by the time you reach the island,
> wealthy with all you have gained on the way . . . .
> (pp. 18-19)

Like the journey to Ithaka, the voyage of Invitational Leadership is one of the spirit, requiring vigilance, continuous learning and continuous exploration. It is a voyage that rewards us with the solitary discoveries we make about ourselves and our ultimate purpose, as well as with the opportunities it affords to collaborate with respected and trusted colleagues on projects of mutual benefit. It is a voyage that returns us again and again to the things that truly matter in this life—relationships with family and friends and associates, as well as connections to the larger communities of which we are part. It is a voyage that carries with it awesome responsibilities and challenges, pushing us always toward exciting new discoveries and accomplishments. Finally, in the most fortunate of circumstances, it is a voyage that allows us to "winter into wisdom" (Heaney, 2001, p. 119) with dignity and grace, wealthy with all we have gained along the way.

REFERENCES

Alberti, R.E., & Emmons, M.L. (1990). *Your Perfect Right: A Guide to Assertive Behavior*. San Louis Obispo, CA: Impact Publishers.

Allen, S. (1982). *More Funny People*. New York: Stein & Day, Publishers.

Arceneaux, C.J. (1994). Trust: An exploration of its nature and significance. Journal of Invitational Theory and Practice, 3, 18-49.

Bacon, J. (1985). *How Sweet It Is: The Jackie Gleason Story*. New York: St. Martin's Press.

Banagi, M.R., & Prentice, D.A. (1994). "The Self in Social Contexts." *Annual Review of Psychology*, 45, 297-332.

Bandura, A. (1994). "Self-Efficacy." In V.S. Ramachaudran (Ed.), *Encyclopedia of Human Behavior* (Vol. 4, 71-81). New York: Academic Press.

Baum, L.F. (Adapted by Horace J. Elias, 1939; renewed, 1976). *The Wizard of Oz*. Metro-Goldwyn-Mayer, Baltimore, MD: Ottenheimer Publishers.

Bellow, Saul (1970). *Mr. Sammler's Planet*. New York: Viking Press.

Bennis, W. (1999). "The Secrets of Great Groups." In F. Hesselbein (Ed.), *Leader to Leader: Enduring Insights on Leadership from the Drucker Foundation's Award-Winning Journal* (pp. 315-322). San Francisco: Jossey-Bass Publishers, Inc.

Bennis, W.G., & Nanus, B. (1985). *Leaders: The Strategies for Taking Charge*. New York: Harper and Row.

Berglas, S. (1985). "Self-handicapping and Self-handicappers: A Cognitive/attributional Model of Interpersonal Self-protective Behavior." In R. Hogan & W.H. Jones (Eds.), *Perspectives in Personality: Theory, Measurement, and Interpersonal Dynamics* (pp. 235-270). Greenwich, CT: JAI Press.

Burns, G. (1976). *George Burns Living It Up or, They Still Love Me in Altoona.* New York: G.P. Putnam and Sons.

Butler, P.E. (1981). *Talking to Yourself: Learning the Language of Self-support.* San Francisco: Harper and Row.

Callahan, S. (1986). *Adrift: Seventy-six Days Lost at Sea.* New York: Ballantine Books.

Calvino, I. (1974). *Invisible Cities.* New York: Harcourt Brace Jovanovich.

Campbell, J.D., Assanand, S., & DiPaula, A. (2000). "Structural Features of the Self Concept and Adjustment. In A. Tesser, R. Felson, & J. Suls (Eds.), *Psychological Perspectives on Self and Identity.* Washington, DC: American Psychological Association.

Castaneda, C. (1972). *A Separate Reality: Further Conversations with Don Juan.* New York: Pocket Books.

Cavafy, C.P. (1972). *Selected Poems* (E. Keeley & P. Sherrard , Trans.). Princeton, New Jersey: Princeton University Press.

Clendenin, J. (1989, January 3). *Reweaving This Country's Unraveling Educational Tapestry* [Keynote Address at The Chancellor's Forum, East Carolina University].

Colby, A., & Ehrlich, T. (2000). "Higher Education and the Development of Civic Responsibility". In T. Ehrlich (Ed.), *Civic Responsibility and Higher Education* (pp. xxi-xliii). Phoenix, AZ: Oyrx Press.

Collins, Jim (2001). *Good to Great: Why Some Companies Make the Leap—and Some Don't.* New York: Harper.

Combs, A.W., Avila, D.L., & Purkey, W.W. (1978). *Helping Relationships: Basic Concepts for the Helping Professions* (2nd ed.). Boston: Allyn and Bacon.

Combs, A.W., & Snygg, D. (1959). *Individual Behavior* (2nd ed.). New York: Harper and Row.

Covey, S. R. (1991). *Principle-Centered Leadership.* New York: Summit Books.

Covey, S.R., Merrill, A.R., & Jones, Dewitt (1998). *The Nature of*

Leadership. Salt Lake City, Utah: Franklin Covey Company.

Covington, M..V. (1992). *Making the Grade: A Self-worth Perspective on Motivation and School Reform*. Cambridge: Cambridge University Press.

Csikszentmihalyi, M. (1990). *Flow: The Psychology of Optimal Experience*. New York: Harper Collins.

Cummings, E.E. (1991). *Complete Poems, 1904-1962*. New York: Liveright Publishing Corporation.

Day, C. (1935). *Life with Father*. New York, London: A.A. Knopf.

Deal, T.E., & Kennedy, A.A. (1985). *Corporate Cultures: The Rites and Rituals of Corporate Life*. Reading, MA: Addison-Wesley.

DePree, M. (1989). *Leadership is an Art*. New York: Doubleday.

De Saint-Exupery, A. (1943). *The Little Prince*. New York: Harcourt, Brace & World.

Dumas, A. (1962). *The Three Musketeers*. New York: MacMillan.

Dunlap, A. (1996). *Mean Business: How I Save Bad Companies and Make Good Companies Great*. MD: Crown Publishing Group, Inc.

Dworkin, A.G., Haney, C.A., Dworkin, R.Jl, & Telschow, R.L. (1990). *Stress and Illness Behavior Among Urban Public School Teachers*. Educational Administration Quarterly, 26, (1), 60-72.

Ellis, A. (1958). *Rational Psychotherapy*. The Journal of General Psychology, 58, 35-49.

Ellis, A. (1976). *Reason and Emotion in Psychotherapy*. New York: Lyle Stuart.

Ellis, A. (1979). "Rational-Emotive Therapy". In R. Corsini (Ed.), *Current Psychotherapies* (pp. 185-229). Itasca, IL: F.E. Peacock.

Eliot, T.S. (1963). *Collected Poems: 1909-1962*. New York: Harcourt Brace.

Fink, D. (2000). *Good Schools/Real Schools: Why School Reform Doesn't Last*. New York: Teachers College Press.

Firestone, R.W. (1997). *Suicide and the Inner Voice*. Thousand Oaks, CA: Sage Publications.

Ford, L. R. (2000). *The Spaces Between Buildings*. Baltimore: John Hopkins University.

Fromm, E. (1956). *The Art of Loving: An Inquiry into the Nature of Love*. New York: Harper & Row.

Fukuyama, F. (1995). *Trust: The Social Virtues and the Creation of Prosperity*. New York: Free Press.

Gill, B. (1975). *Here at the New Yorker*. New York: Random House, Inc.

Gilligan, C. (1982). *In a Different Voice*. Cambridge, MA: Harvard University Press.

Gladwell, M. (2000). *The Tipping Point: How Little Things Can Make a Big Difference*. New York: Little, Brown and Company.

Goleman, D. (2002). *Primal Leadership: Realizing the Power of Emotional Intelligence*. Cambridge: Harvard Business School Press.

Greenleaf, R.K. (2002). "Essentials of Servant-leadership." In L.C. Spears & M. Lawrence (Eds.), *Focus on Leadership: Servant-leadership for the 21st Century* (pp. 19-25). New York: John Wiley & Sons, Inc.

Greenleaf, R.K. (1996). "The Strategies of a Leader". In D.M. Frick & L.C. Spears (Eds.), *On becoming a Servant Leader: The Private Writings of Robert K. Greenleaf* (pp.299-311). San Francisco: Jossey-Bass Publishers, Inc.

Guba, E.C. (1990). "The Alternative Paradigm Dialog." In E.C. Guba (Ed.), *The Paradigm Dialog* (pp.17-30). Thousand Oaks, CA: Sage Publications.

Halberstam, D. (1986). *The Reckoning*. New York: Bantam Books.

Harrington, Rev. F. (1993, January 16). *American Heroes—Where are They? Who are They?* Peachtree Presbyterian Pulpit.

Harris. M.J. (1989). *The Zanucks of Hollywood: The Dark Legacy of an American Dynasty*. Toronto: Stoddart Publishing.

Hay, P. (1990). *Movie Anecdotes*. New York: Oxford University Press.

Heaney, S. (2001). *Beowulf: A New Verse Translation*. New York: W.W. Norton & Company.

Helmstetter, S. (1986). *What to Say When You Talk to Yourself: The Major New Breakthrough to Managing People, Yourself, and Success*. Scottsdale, Arizona: Grindle Press.

Hesselbein, F (1999). "Introduction". In F. Hesselbein (Ed.), *Leader to Leader: Enduring Insights from the Drucker Foundation's Award-winning Journal* (pp. xi-xiv). San Francisco: Jossey-Bass Publishers, Inc.

Hyams, J. (1979). *Zen in the Martial Arts*. New York: Bantam Books.

Hymowitz, K. (2001). *Ecstatic Capitalism's Brave New Work Ethic.* City Journal, 11 (1), 32-43.

James, W. (1890). *Principles of Psychology* (Vols. 1-2). Magnolia, MA: Peter Smith.

Joyce, J. (1964). *A Portrait of the Artist as a Young Man.* New York: Viking Press.

Kanin, G. (1974). *Hollywood.* New York: Viking Press.

Kesey, K. (1962). *One Flew Over the Cookoo's Nest.* New York: Viking Press.

Kiecolt-Glaser, J.K., Garner, W., Speicher, C., Penn, G.M., Holliday, J., & Glaser, R. (1984a). *Psychosocial Modifiers of Immunocompetence in Medical Students.* Psychosomatic Medicine, 46, 7-14.

Kiecolt-Glaser, J.K., Ricker, D., Messick, G., Speicher, C.E., Garner, W., & Glaser, R. (1984b). *Urinary Cortisol, Cellular Immunocompetency and Loneliness in Psychiatric Impatients.* Psychosomatic Medicine, 46, 15-24.

Kindel, S., & Loeb, Marshall (1999). *Leadership for Dummies.* Indianapolis: Hungry Minds, Inc.

Kingsweel, M. (1994). *Citizenship and Civility: The True North Strong and Free, Thank You.* University of Toronto Magazine, 22 (20), 14-19.

Kouzes, J.M. (1999). "Finding Your Leadership Voice." In F. Hesselbein (Ed.), *Leader to Leader: Enduring Insights from the Drucker Foundation's Award-winning Journal.* San Francisco: Jossey-Bass Publishers, Inc.

Kouzes, J.M., & Posner, B.R. (1995). *The Leadership Challenge: How to Keep Getting Extraordinary Things Done in Organizations.* San Francisco: Jossey-Bass Publishers, Inc.

Lindbergh, A.M. (1955). *Gift from the Sea.* New York: Pantheon.

Malone, D. (1973). *Thomas Jefferson: The Man, his World, and Influence.* New York: G.P. Putnam & Sons.

Marcus, B., & Blank, A. (1999). *Built from Scratch: How a Couple of Regular Guys Grew the Home Depot from Nothing to $30 billion.* New York: Times Books.

Markus, H., & Nurius, P. (1986). *Possible Selves.* American Psychologist, 41 (9), 954-969.

Marquez, G.G. (1988). *Love in the Time of Cholera.* New York: Alfred

Knopf.

Maslow, A.H. (1954). *Motivation and Personality*. New York: Harper and Row.

Masters, E.L. (1986). *Spoon River Anthology*. New York: Buccaneer Books.

Maugham, W.S. (1944). *The Razor's Edge*. New York: Doubleday.

May, R. (1969). *Love and Will*. New York: W.W. Norton & Co., Inc.

Mead, G.H. (1934). *Mind, Self and Society*. Chicago: University of Chicago Press.

Meichenbaum, D. (1977). *Cognitive-Behavior Modification: An Integrative Approach*. New York: Plenum.

Meichenbaum, D. (1985). *Stress Inoculation Training*. New York: Pergamon Press.

Miline, A.A. (1926). *Winnie the Pooh*. New York: E.P. Dutton.

Morris, V.C. (1966). *Existentialism in Education: What it Means*. New York: Harper and Row.

Neumann, A. (1995). *Context, Cognition, and Culture: A Case Analysis of Collegiate Leadership and Cultural Change*. American Educational Research Journal. 32 (2). 251-279.

Noddings, N. (1984). *Caring: A Feminine Approach to Ethics and Moral Education*. Berkely: University of California Press.

Ouchi, W.G. (1981). *Theory Z: How American Business Can Meet the Japanese Challenge*. Reading, MA: Addison-Wesley.

Patton, G.S., Jr. (1947). *War as I Knew It*. New York: Houghton Mifflin.

Percy, Walker (1961). *The Moviegoer*. New York: Random House.

Percy, Walker (1980). *The Second Coming*. New York: Farrar, Straus & Giroux.

Peters, T.J., & Waterman, R.H., Jr. (1982). *In Search of Excellence: Lessons from America's Best Run Companies*. New York: Harper and Row.

Pierce, T. (1995). *Leading Out Loud: The Authentic Speaker, the Credible Leader*. San Francisco: Jossey-Bass Publishers.

Pines, A.M., & Aronson, E. (with Ditsa Kafry). (1981). Burnout: From Tedium to Personal Growth. New York: Free Press.

Podemski, R.S. & Childers, J.H., Jr. (1991). *How to Deal with Angry People: Human Relations Strategies That Work*. Journal of Educational Public Relations 14 (3), 31-33.

Prather, H. (1970). *Notes to Myself*. Lafayette, CA: Real People Press.

Robbins, T. (1976). *Even Cowgirls Get the Blues.* New York: Houghton-Mifflin.

Rogers, C.R. (1974). *In Retrospect: Forty-Six Years.* American Psychologist, 29, 115.

Rosenblatt, R. (1982). *The Man in the Water.* Time (Jan. 25, 1982); 86.

Ross, R. (1996). *Returning to the Teachings: Exploring Aboriginal Justice.* Ontario: Penguin.

Russell, L. (date not given). *How to Win Friends, Kick Ass, and Influence People.* VA: Saint Martin's Press, LLC.

Sandburg, C. (1948). *Remembrance Rock.* New York: Harcourt Brace.

Schaub, A.R. (1991). *The Power of Poor Communication.* Journal of Educational Public Relations, 14, 3.

Scheier, M.F., & Carver, C.S. (1992). *On the Power of Positive Thinking: The Benefits of Being Optimistic.* Current Directions in Psychological Science, 1, 26-30.

Schultz, C. (1968). *Peanuts.* New York: United Features Syndicate, Inc.

Schwartz, D. (1967). *Selected Poems (1938-1958): Summer knowledge.* New York: New Directions.

Seligman, M.E. (1975). *Helplessness: On Depression, Development, and Death.* San Francisco: W.H. Freeman.

Seligman, M.E.P. (1990). *Learned Optimism.* New York: Alfred A. Knopf.

Sessa, V., & Taylor, J. (2000). *Executive Selection: Strategies for Success.* San Francisco: Jossey-Bass.

Silvers, P. (with Saffron, R.) (1973). *The Laugh is on Me: The Phil Silvers Story.* Englewood Cliffs, New Jersey: Prentice-Hall, Inc.

Smith, B. (1943). *A Tree Grows in Brooklyn.* New York, London: Harper and Brothers.

Sokolov, A.N. (1972). *Inner Speech and Thought.* New York: Plenum Press.

Stoll, L., & Fink, D. (1996). *Changing our Schools, Linking School Effectiveness and School Improvement.* Buckingham, UK: Open University Press.

Swindoll, C. (1983). *Growing Strong in the Seasons of Life.* Grand Rapids, Michigan: Zondervan Publishing House.

Taylor, R.L. (1967). *W.C. Fields: His Follies and Fortunes.* New York: Signet Books.

Tichy, N. (1997). *The Leadership Rngine: How Winning Companies Build Leaders at Every Level.* New York: Harperbusiness.

Tsunetomo, Y. (1979). Hagakure: *The Book of the Samurai.* Tokyo: Kodanshi International.

Tyler, Anne (1982). *Dinner at the Homesick Restaurant.* New York: Alfred A. Knopf, Inc.

Vygotsky, L.S. (1978). *Mind in Society: The Development of Higher Psychological Processes.* Cambridge: Harvard University Press.

Wagoner, J.L., Jr. (1976). *Thomas Jefferson and the Education of a New Nation.* Bloomington, Indiana: Phi Delta Kappa Educational Foundation.

Waitley, D. (1995). *Empires of the Mind.* New York: William Morrow and Co.

Warner, O. (1976). *Command at Sea: Great Fighting Admirals from Hawke to Nimitz.* New York: St. Martin's Press.

Wheatley, M.J. (1992). *Leadership and the New Science.* San Francisco: Barrett-Koehler Publishers.

Wiemer, D.D., & Purkey, W.W. (1994). *Love Thyself as Thy Neighbor? Self-other Orientations of Inviting Behaviors.* Journal of Invitational Theory and Practice, 3, (1), 25-33.

Wright, F.L. (1954). *The Natural House.* New York: Horizon Press.

Wurman, R.S. (1989). *Information Anxiety.* New York: Doubleday.

ABOUT THE AUTHORS

Dr. Betty L. Siegel heads Kennesaw State University which has been cited as a "college on the move" by Jossey-Bass and labeled a "rising star" among regional universities in the south by U.S. News and World Report. KSU has received national recognition for its Freshman Year Experience programs, its new Living/Learning Communities, and its emphasis on leadership development for students, faculty and staff.

Named Cobb County Citizen of the Year in 1996 and "Georgia Woman of the Year" in 1997, Dr. Siegel was inducted into the Atlanta Business Hall of Fame in 1999. She has been repeatedly cited among Georgia Trend magazine's list of 100 most influential Georgians. She has served on six corporate boards, and presently sits on numerous community service boards. A long time member of the American Association of State Colleges and Universities, she served as chair of the Board of Directors, and she is a long-time member of the Business Higher Education Forum.

As a result of her leadership among state educators and commitment to community service, Dr. Siegel was appointed to the

Governor's Delegation representing Governor Zell Miller at the 1997 President's Summit on America's Future. Governor Miller also chose her to represent the State of Georgia on the Southern Growth Policies Board's 1998 Commission on the Future of the South.

As an internationally and nationally known lecturer and speaker on leadership, Dr. Siegel has delivered keynote addresses at hundreds of national, regional, and state conferences throughout the fifty states, Puerto Rico, and ten foreign countries. She has also served as a consultant to educational, business, not-for profit organizations, health services, government, and civic groups. In addition, she has lectured at more than 100 colleges and universities around the world.

Dr. William Watson Purkey is Professor of Counseling and Development at the University of North Carolina at Greensboro. An active writer, lecturer, researcher and leader, Dr. Purkey has authored or co-authored over 90 professional articles and nine books. His professional experience includes teaching in the public school system, as a university professor, a college administrator, and as an Explosive Ordnance Disposal Specialist in the United State Air Force.

Dr. Purkey has keynoted hundreds of national and international conferences. His ability to invite others to the celebration of leading, learning, and living is reflected in his many awards for teaching, including the highest award for teaching given by the University of North Carolina University System, The Board of Governors Award for Excellence in Teaching.

Drs. Siegel and Purkey are co-founders and co-directors of the International Alliance for Invitational Education, a non-profit organization chartered in North Carolina in 1982. In 1999 Drs. Siegel and Purkey created the Center for Invitational Leadership. This center advances the model of invitational education by offering opportunities for professionals to participate in leadership development programs.

Printed in the United States
140954LV00004B/2/A